Independent Music Promo

YOUR BAND IS A VIRUS!

by

James Moore

Behind-The-Scenes & Viral Marketing for the Independent Musician

"YOUR BAND IS A VIRUS" is © 2012 Independent Music Promotions
All rights reserved worldwide
First Edition 2010
No part of this publication may be stored in a retrieval system, transmitted, or reproduced in any way, including, but not limited to digital copying, without the prior agreement and written permission of the publisher.

Independent Music Promotions

Promote your band at
www.independentmusicpromotions.com

Independent Music Promotions

Table of Contents

Introduction
Types of Marketing
Your Image
Build a Website
Newsletters and Mailing Lists
Viral Marketing
How to Sell
Myspace
More strategies
Podcasts
Music Mp3 Blogs
Guerrilla Marketing
Branding
Resources
Bonus Interview with Stuart Epps

Introduction

Welcome to "YOUR BAND IS A VIRUS". If you're reading this then it means you've decided to take a chance on a different kind of music marketing e-book. Why is it different? Well, first of all, a record label CEO or music industry mogul did not write this book. Gathering the top strategies, tactics and opinions from the soldiers on the frontlines – the independent musicians, is what put this book together.

The idea behind the title "YOUR BAND IS A VIRUS" is a mindset. If you can get into that mindset and get inspired about promoting your band, you're on the right track and this will help you with the work that's ahead.

And you can bet there will be work. Let's be realistic. If you're not enthused about working hard to expose your music to more people, no one else will be. You may as well stay in your room and play your acoustic if you're not willing to log the hours. So get excited and get ready to start building your band's public profile in a big way.

Your band is, in fact, a virus.

Every product, art piece or idea in our modern society can be related to this concept. This means that while an idea or product can certainly spread quickly amongst the general public, some methods are much more effective than others. Spam, for example, is an advertising method that many potential customers have built up immunity to, and it is therefore a poor choice to utilize for bands trying to promote themselves. The goal for the independent musician is to find creative ways to get more and more people to "catch" their virus, and also to create multiple ways for the virus to spread with ease.

In "YOUR BAND IS A VIRUS", we will attempt to provide something not offered by many other "Independent band guides" or "Independent marketing e-books". It's going to be in plain English. Less filler. Less rambling. NO stories.

Now we're not out to name any names here, but have you purchased or read any other music marketing e-books?

How many cartoons did you see taking up half the space of the respective books? Chances are the images of someone madly typing away at a keyboard didn't help you much with your promotional efforts, right? I figured that.

How many stories and examples of successful promotional campaigns did you read? Did you scour through the books only to find endless stories and not enough relevant, actionable content?

We've read the same books in our search for the best tactics to promote ourselves with. Some books are filled with story after story – "Band A from New York decided to send out free chocolate bars (or insert other item that you would NEVER in a million years send) with their promo packages."

(This story could take up 3 pages as you search it frantically for relevance to your own band.)

While this style of writing can definitely provide some helpful ideas and get the creative process going, it can also be somewhat insulting to pay for a marketing book, and finish it with very little to work with as far as real-life scenarios.

We know that what works for a pop artist will simply not work for a death metal band. An acoustic performer can perform at the local bookstore, but the hard core punk band cannot. Therefore, there's simply no need for a book filled solely with examples, particularly ones regarding giving out sweets of any kind. We assume that you are all creative people and you will have no trouble thinking of more powerful and compelling ways to put the ideas in this book to good use.

It's the philosophy and the thinking behind independent music marketing, and success, for that matter, that needs to change. Independent musicians have reduced themselves to a horde of spammers, unable to communicate with their potential fan bases or tap into modern marketing practises. To prove this point, when was the last time you checked out a band who sent you an email saying "CHECK US OUT!!!" or "Saw you were a fan of (insert band name here). We thought you would like our stuff." I`m sure you never have. So to any of you bands who just realized that this fits your description to a tee, you can safely stop spamming now and approach the music industry with some dignity!

Here's a newsflash for the modern marketing plan.

You don't ALWAYS need to pay someone.

Why should independent musicians be the one singled-out group in the music industry who pay out of their pockets for everything, but get peanuts in return? Are we meant to be a laughing stock? Do we have to look desperate and in need to the industry and the music listeners? Paying for promotional services and coverage should be a part of our marketing plan, but not all of it! It's time to make some changes to our approach, to advance and empower ourselves. Let's get our music to the frontlines with honest practises and ignore the dinosaur-like mentality that dominates the industry.

Don't pay to wait in line or get put on a list.

Independent Music Promotions

The whole idea of this book is to give you as many helpful tools as possible to work with in the promotion of your music. There will be a good deal that you can use immediately. No need to read the book front to back. Work on it one tactic at a time if you like. The format of the book will all revolve around actual advice you can use.

Another few points to make: this book will focus mainly on online promotion of your music. Why? Well, for one, advice on booking tours, getting a manager, and making your way through the music business can be found in other fine books such as "Confessions of a Record Producer" by Moses Avalon. And plus, it all starts online. You need to build the foundation online, and why not make it a strong one?

Let's try to also keep our expectations reasonable. What you get out of the tools described in this book will depend strongly on how you use them. You may find that some promotional tactics work better for you than others. Expect your hard work to advance you and gain new fans, more hits to your website, more downloads of your music, and more press coverage. These things taken far enough will give you a strong reputation and poise you for bigger successes.

Some bands have gotten signed from online promotion and viral tactics alone, while some bands don't want to bother going near a computer. Unless your uncle is the CEO of EMI, or your band is making it to the top of the Los Angeles club circuit, you will need some serious online promotion on your side. It's all up to you and how hard you want to work at it.

We're going to try some methods not commonly used by today's breed of independent artists, such as **Viral Marketing**, **Guerrilla marketing** and **Behind-the-scenes marketing**.

Well, they say "It's all in the meat", so let's get right to it.

Types of Marketing

Guerrilla Marketing

According to Wikipedia, *"Guerrilla marketing is an unconventional system of promotions that relies on time, energy and imagination rather than a big marketing budget. Typically, guerrilla marketing tactics are unexpected and unconventional; consumers are targeted in unexpected places, which can make the idea that's being marketed memorable, generate buzz, and even spread virally."*

This is ideal and this is one of our main goals. Get creative with all the ideas and tactics described in this book. Talk to people individually. Different tactics will work for different publications and individuals.

Independent musicians must be relentless and innovative with their marketing in order to achieve any level of success. Don't be afraid of doing things differently, so long as it works. There is no one rule.

Remember the examples rule: What works for a metal band may not work for a classical violinist. Each musician has their own niche, their own angle to exploit and use to their advantage. Chances are if you try to follow exactly what works for another band, it won't work. You need something that is your own.

Much of Guerilla marketing is about capturing attention with your tactic – doing things radically differently from the mainstream, and potentially your competitors as well. Make sure it works for your band since this is an individual thing.

And keep in mind Guerilla marketing has nothing to do with spamming, which will hurt more than help, or generic advertising, which currently has a fairly small effect in the online marketplace. Guerilla marketing means aggressively reaching out to and covering your potential markets while leaving no stone unturned. Make sure your tentacles reach everywhere necessary!

Sound good? Ok, now for the next tactic.

Behind-the-Scenes Marketing

Behind-the-Scenes marketing is the tactic of manoeuvring behind the scenes to create a positive or powerful image for the buying public.

For example, and we will discuss this in further detail later, contacting and befriending an individual writer at a music magazine and convincing him to review your band. Sure, HE knows that you looked him up and that you are an independent band desperately in need of coverage, but all the public sees is a good review on the next big thing. And the more you do this, the bigger and better you look. This will become one of the most important parts of your strategy to create a "frontline" image for your band.

Behind-the-Scenes marketing is all about making connections from nothing, making those connections work for you by being personal, and using the results to leverage yourself against your competition.

That's the way it should be, right?

Viral Marketing

What is Viral marketing? According to Wikipedia, viral marketing refers to marketing techniques that use social networks to produce increases in brand awareness or to achieve other marketing objectives. It compares viral marketing to the spread of a computer virus.

The main idea is that, as a strategy, simply marketing with generic advertisements ("You need this" style of marketing) is on the extreme downswing, and in fact is barely working at all in some markets.

Viral marketing is all about getting people to sell and advertise for you.

Get your product talked about in the social networks, websites, forums, and blogs - and watch the magic happen. You no longer have anything to do with it. We'll go over a host of viral ideas in another chapter.

Your Image

Record your music right

Remember when we said we want to keep this book potent and advice-based? As mundane as it sounds, we need to go over this point. If your music is not professional quality yet, **THIS IS THE FIRST STEP!** Make sure you prepare your best tracks and record a professional CD or series of tracks to promote yourself with. It's an obvious point – but the music must be intact. Don't rush the process in order to get online faster. Pay the money and get it recorded right. The market is already flooded with bands that have extremely high quality production. Being at their level is **only the starting point** and it's the bare minimum you need to succeed in the music business. You may be able to score a great deal by recording in a home studio or with a music production student. The main thing is to have strong material that is recorded well. Not necessarily Michael Jackson quality of course, but it must be impressive!

There's nothing worse than going to a band's MySpace page and hearing garage or ghetto blaster quality recordings. It's a waste of everyone's time. If this sounds like your band, take your mp3's down temporarily until you re-record. Then you'll be ready to start promoting. Even if you get 3 songs properly recorded, it's better than a full album of ghetto blaster noise. No one in the industry expects a 15 song album these days. Some bands choose to release an mp3 per month, or a 4 song digital release. All the rules have been broken, so do what's right for your band.

If you are unprepared financially to record even one song professionally, go make some money and make it happen. How will you do anything else if you can't do this? You should not be listed **ANYWHERE** on the internet with unprofessional content representing you – even on local websites and forums. If everyone followed this advice, independent music websites would be much more popular, and much more rewarding to scour through. Imagine MySpace without all the amateur garbage?

Get content

What do we mean by content? Well, you have your CD recorded and you want to get started with online promotion. You will need at least a biography, some artwork, and some professionally done photos.

Biography

For the biography, keep it fairly short and without language such as "The Evil Lizards are the best band to come out of North America since Metallica." As great as this statement sounds, it will just end up making you look like jerks. It will not have the desired effect (Metallica fans and media personnel foaming at the mouth to check out your music). As you gain press (which we'll get to) you can also add press quotes to your bio. Why?

Because it's ok for **OTHER PEOPLE** to brag about you – but you can't do it yourself. Remember that!

It's also ok and even recommended to talk about your influences in your band's biography. Until you're as big as U2, go ahead and mention who influenced your sound. As long as it's done in the correct way, it will definitely entice more people to give your music a chance, and also help your search engine results, successfully tying your band name to the influences of your choice. Just be sure to keep it accurate and information based.

For example:

"Inspired by the likes of Tool, Metallica, Queens of the Stone Age and Lamb of God, the Evil Lizards showcase their own aggressive brand of metal-infused rock music."

The reason a statement like this would work well is because the band is mentioning some very successful bands as a tribute of sorts, while not making the language overly promotional. This quote is meant to entice fans of the aforementioned bands to wonder, "What do the Evil

Lizards sound like? If they sound anything like a cross between Tool, Metallica and Queens of the Stone Age, they must be awesome!"

Sample Band Biography

Here's a sample band biography to help you. Remember, the bio is for the media, the music industry, future contacts as well as your fans. It should read like a fact sheet, but keep it creative, energetic and useful. Be sure it represents your band. Make them want to listen:

Independent Music Promotions

1st Paragraph:

You will need an introduction. This should be a sentence that clearly defines you, your band name or alias, where you're from, your specific genre of music (eclectic brand of space rock, punk-infused speed metal – make it interesting but don't lie!), etc. You can also add a positive quote you have received from a website, blog, radio or magazine review. (Rock Magazine calls the Sonic Spacemen "A real rock juggernaut…the sound of the future".)

2nd Paragraph:

This paragraph will go over the purpose of the bio. What is your band up to? If you have a new CD coming out, this should be the topic of the paragraph. Promotional information such as tours, events or music videos to support the album should also be mentioned here.

3rd and 4th Paragraphs:

Relevant information on band members (edit out the bit about your drummer being the greatest player since Danny Carrey!), band accomplishments (festival spots, glowing reviews, etc), experience (tours), and information about the forming of the band can be delved into here.

Ending:

Summarize current activities and events, the goals of the band, and be sure to include another raving press quote here.

Band artwork

The artwork you choose will represent your band, so make sure it's strong and consistent with your message and style. There are many independent and professional graphic designers who will create custom art to help you stand out from the crowd. If you are talented in the area of graphic design, do it yourself! If you want to learn, there are plenty of courses available, as well as online tutorials on graphic design. This is where having no rules can help you. For some artists, even hand drawn or very low quality art suits their image perfectly. Remember, music fans check out new bands in many cases because of interesting or intriguing artwork, whether it's a CD cover or a band logo.

Band photos

For photos, there should be plenty of amateur, yet professional and ambitious photographers in your area who are looking to photograph bands for a small fee and are happy to provide you with the high quality photos in return for credit (Photo taken by _____), or a small fee. Sometimes student photographers will take pictures of bands for free simply for experience or word-of-mouth promotion. With the improvement of quality of digital cameras, photos can also be done yourself or by someone in your circle of friends. Try to do something eye catching and original with your band promo shots, but keep it professional.

Remember, these will represent you on your website, and also be used in the media when you are interviewed, reported on or reviewed. Taking photos on your cell phone or cheap camera is not going to cut it. Hire someone who is serious about photography and trying to build their portfolio (hint: they will give you a deal.)

Another important tip about getting photos for your band – Take it seriously and dress appropriately. This doesn't necessarily mean you need to wear a suit. You must make it suit your music though. Consider the band photos you see from the millions of bands flooding the market today. Jeans and t-shirts, right? It's up to you, but the "show up in your street clothes" approach just doesn't seem like an eye-catching option anymore in today's option overloaded marketplace.

The band's that will stand out in the new marketplace are the ones who have an image. The ones who are daring enough to be different will succeed. Whether this means that your band dresses up in army fatigues, Alice in Wonderland costumes, crimson robes, suits, tribal attire, masks, or zombie makeup, you've simply got to do something to stand out in the crowd.

Think about it this way. How would you dress to your sister's wedding? How would you dress if you were to have a meeting with your idol? How about if you were to perform a work of art that is very dear to you?

If music is unimportant to you – stop! If it IS important to you, discard your subconscious negativities and give it the respect it deserves. Dress appropriately. Now this may be an extreme example, but I was perusing a local music magazine this morning. It seemed every independent band I came across were posing in supermarket aisles, lying in a field, or pushing each other around in a shopping cart with big smiles on their faces. Guess how many of these bands intrigued me with a sense of mystique, or even honesty? None. I assumed right away that their music was terrible. Then I came across a feature article on the metal band Behemoth. Even if I did not listen to metal, I would admit it's an extremely effective image, and I might just listen to their music out of curiosity.

Ok, now that you have your music professionally recorded and you've got some slick looking content, you're ready to....

Build a Website

Here is another obvious one. Yes, you can start off with a simple MySpace profile and start the website later (Just try not to let this go on for long). You WILL need your own domain (such as www.bestbandever.com) before you decide to release your CD. This is for a few reasons.

It makes you look more professional. If you use it properly, the official website will push you ahead of the "MySpace horde". Having your own website allows you to be taken more seriously, and also shows the industry that you have your "ducks in a row".

It gives your band a more 'permanent' image than a band with only a MySpace. Having a strong website really demonstrates commitment and potential staying power. It shows that your intention is to last a long time.

It's a home base to market your product (your CD's and merchandise) and customize your e-store. It's your home base, free of outside voices (except the ones YOU approve). Give people something exciting and a reason to visit again.

Better sound quality options than sites such as MySpace. People may check you out on MySpace for a preview of your sound. But MySpace sound quality is quite poor. It's notoriously poor, in fact. An official website will give you options for higher quality previews of your music.

Mailing list capability, membership options, E-team registration, free downloads and other promotion, design and marketing options.

Get people involved in your official website. Make it a destination place for people to frequent online. Create incentives to encourage people to sign up for your website, e-team or mailing list. We'll expand on this later.

How do you build a website?

Well, the good news is you don't really need to know how to build a website – or at least not by any html method.

First you'll want to buy your domain at a hosting website such as www.godaddy.com. There are many reasons why to stick with a .com or a .net address. Some people may be unsure about whether to visit your website or not if it has a strange or unknown address. It's simply easier for people to find you and it's the most **trustworthy and recognizable** way to do it.

So if your ideal address **www.evillizards.com** is taken, try out **www.evillizards.net, www.evillizardsband.com** or **www.evillizardsmusic.com**. Make sure it is easy to remember and makes sense for your band.

Next you can get a cheap hosting account at sites such as www.hostgator.com and then build your site from there. If you are familiar with html, you'll be ready to customize your official website with no trouble. If you're unfamiliar with doing it yourself, you'll require some help along the way.

One option is to hire a professional web designer. If you've got original ideas for your website and want to stand out from the crowd, this could be the way to go. Just don't get too ambitious. Remember, your website will be like your press package. You don't need all the bells and whistles. Just the necessities.

Don't spend too much on web design.

The days of spending $1,000 or more on custom websites are long gone. There are MUCH better ways that you can spend $1,000 on your music career than getting a website done.

For every web designer who offers to charge you $1,000 for a quality website there will be ten who offer you $250. Shop around and don't hesitate to hire an ambitious student. Students need the extra cash and can do a great job. Also, make sure that the web designer knows how to create a mailing list template (or insert a pre-existing one for you), and design a website according to the marketing criteria that you'll require as an independent musician trying to advance yourself.

If you want to build the site yourself and be in control of everything – I don't blame you. And the good news is that you can certainly do it.

There are two popular ways to do this. Both options are reputable and roughly the same price. Both offer custom website designs that bands and artists can individualize with their own art and photos. They both also offer high storage space for music and media. Mailing lists, e-store capability, blogs, and forums are other features both sites offer. You will definitely need these features in order to effectively promote your band online.

If you decide to go this route, check out the links below and decide for yourself. We have had good experiences with both companies, but Bandzoogle would get our recommendation for a superior administration, better template options and many more extensive features offered, especially for the amateur or inexperienced webmaster:

www.bandzoogle.com

www.hostbaby.com

What should you put on your website?

Well, you can get creative but there are some things that your website must have. First, the big 3:

The Main Page – This is the first thing visitors to your site will typically see. **Do not set up a splash or intro page!** This will drive away more people than it will entice. Your main page should include a brief introduction so people know what site they are on. It can have a news section. It's also a good idea to have a sidebar with option to sign up for your mailing list or e-team.

The Music page – Post your music on this page (obviously). Don't be a prude with the sound samples and previews. 30-second previews are a thing of the past and they will make you look like a chump. Be generous. Offer a few free downloads or a bunch. Give people something to take with them and **spread virally**. Brief information on the album and a few press clippings can be on this page too provided they don't take too much space.

Buy the CD or Checkout page – This is the most important page of your website. You *do* want to sell, don't you? Your whole website should be based around getting people from the main page to the music page and then to your e-store page. There are other necessary elements of a band's website but these are the 3 most important. The other categories can even be subsections (accessible by drop-down menus) of these 3.

Now for the other pieces of the puzzle:

The Bio: Let people know your band story. Make it available to the press and the fans. Keep it concise and engaging.

Contact: People need to know how to get a hold of you. Make it clear and easy. You don't want to miss any opportunities or questions from fans.

Photos: Post your professional press photos and live photos here. Make sure they're good ones and don't post too many. 10 great shots work much better than 200 live shots taken by your deadbeat uncle. Keep it clean and slick looking!

Mailing list: Put this on your main page, and ideally every page on your website. This will continually remind people that there is a way to keep up to date with all the happenings of your band. This can be as important as a CD sale. Let your network grow.

Blog: Blog away on Wordpress or Blogger. What's your story? What are your opinions? Are you funny? Want to write some music reviews of your own? (This is a great way to use relevant keywords and attract new visitors to your website.) Why not post song lyrics or unreleased material? Make it interesting and engaging. Make people want to come back and check out what you're going to say next. It's also important to spread your blog posts around with the use of keywords and RSS feeds. If the music blogs don't cover you, why not covertly start your own blog?

Press: This is where you post your extensive list of press quotes and accolades. You'll want to do this with permission from the media in question of course. Post links to every piece of press you get. Also, be sure to post interviews with the band. Keep this page full of content. Make it impressive. This will be no trouble once you start reaching out to the music media in the right way.

Links: There are different opinions on whether to have a links section or not, and it's really up to you. It is a good thing to have if you want something to barter with.

Offering banner exchanges or a link exchange is a great form of cross-promotion. Link exchanges with other bands can get you more fans. Basically, at the independent level you will want to get on as many websites as possible, and link exchanges are one of the best ways to do it. Want a good place to start? Try the Indie Bible link exchange at http://www.indiebible.com/ile/index.shtml

Selling as the focus of your website: The two main points to launching your music website are to:

a) Spread your music across the globe.
b) To sell.

That is exactly why the information you provide about yourself should be clean and somewhat minimal, while **the focus of the website should be on your products** (your CD and merchandise).

When you buy a custom t-shirt on EBay, do you care who made it? Do you want to know the company biography? Probably not. You have to present your CD as a product, because this is what people will want to buy. You'll simply cause confusion if you make yourself the main attraction and keep your store hidden away. People can't rent you out. They are buying something you have created.

Don't worry! This is not to say that no one is going to check out your photos or your biography page. You will certainly have fans who are interested in knowing every little thing about you. We're just saying that the best way to set up your website is to focus on selling your products. How are they going to get to your products if your website is overly jammed up with too many photos of you, a guestbook filled with comments from your family, and a 3-page biography covering everything since the first jam?

Sometimes more is less, and extra content can actually work against you, making you look amateur and unprofessional. It's much better to create a mystique than to reveal yourself as a desperate, starving artist – even if that's what you are. No one needs to know. Get out of the way and let them get the products!

Give them a straight path!

Get your Music Online

Now that you have your website up with your samples, now you want people to discover you and buy your music. There are quite a few ways to do this. One of the most obvious things to do is to sign up for Reverbnation (if you haven't done so already). Even though Reverbnation is flooded with bands, many music fans and industry people use it to look for new music.

ITunes is another service you should sign up with. But hold on a minute. Signing up straight through iTunes can be sticky. They are fussy about their database and entries can take a long time to be accepted…but there IS a way around it and we suggest it wholeheartedly.

SIGN UP FOR CDBABY!

Keep in mind that we are an independent organization and are in no way affiliated with CDBaby. That being said, it's simply a great service and one of the best ways for independent artists to actually start to sell product. They were built from the bottom up with independent artists in mind. The reason they are thriving is because their formula works.

Here's how CDBaby.com works:

1. You send CDBaby your CDs and they take care of the rest for you — they process the orders and ship the goods on your behalf. Just add links to CDBaby on your website to make them either your main payment option or a secondary option when people visit your online store.

To kick things off, fill out their submission form at

http://members.cdbaby.com/signup/

They will need to know some basic information about your band and your CD release. Mail them five CDs or more to start.

Independent Music Promotions

2. CDBaby.com will make a Web page specifically to showcase your CD on their Web site.

It includes sound clips, links back to your own Web site, reviews, and all of the text and descriptions you want. You fill in the details and decide what gets posted. Be sure to include lots of relevant keywords to attract new visitors to your CDBaby sales page.

They give this page a simple Web address where you can tell people to buy your CD (www.cdbaby.com/yourname/). They then put it in the listings and search engines at CDBaby.com — a site which gets over 150,000 hits a day from music fans that are looking for new independent CDs to buy. Many of the artists we've worked with have benefited greatly and generated their first sales from CDBaby.com.

3. There is a one-time $35 charge to set up a new CD in their store. It doesn't matter how many CD's you sell. They will not charge you any further fees or remove your CD from the database at any time.

4. CDBaby takes all credit card orders for your CD, online or through their toll-free phone number, and ships it to customers within hours. They e-mail you every time your CD is sold to tell you who bought it. "Break out the champagne" is the phrase.

They also provide the person's email address, **which you should keep track of and add to your mailing list** (important tip). You set your selling price at whatever you want. CDBaby.com keeps $4 per CD sold. Just be sure not to bargain bin yourself or price yourself out of the market.

5. The CDBaby.com deal is non-exclusive. There are no contracts to sign. CDBaby.com is not a record label or a publisher. It's only a record store.

6. You don't need a UPC barcode to sell at CDBaby. Though if you do have one already, they will report your sales to SoundScan! **You don't need to have your CDs shrink-wrapped**.

You can even sell a homemade CD-R there as long as it's presentable (But please get your CD's professionally pressed!)

You don't need to upload mp3 files or send them graphics or anything else. Just fill out their submission form at

http://members.cdbaby.com/signup/

and send them five CDs. They do the rest.

You will be able to manage your CDBaby Web site through their online member area. Anyhow, enough about that. The site simply works, and here's a bonus.

CRITICAL POINT:

Remember we mentioned iTunes and how it's a difficult service to get into? If you sign up for CDBaby, **just opt into their digital distribution program** (also free) **and you will automatically get listed in iTunes, as well as eMusic, Rhapsody, Amazon, Napster, PayPlay, Ruckus and a few others.**

So now you have your CD pressed (we're assuming this because you'll need your product for online promotion), your content (bio and photos) professionally done, and you've set up your website, MySpace profile and CDBaby accounts. Your music is also being showcased at the most popular digital services such as iTunes and Amazon.com.

So now you're on the verge, right? No. This is where most bands go completely wrong. They think that they will record an album, get some photos done, put up a website, and become big stars. The truth is, and this is true for any website or business, if you have a website but don't promote it, you don't have a website. If you have a product but don't advertise it, you have no product. You don't exist! So the most important thing to focus on is how to begin "existing" as a product in the public eye.

Let's look at the positive. You now have the groundwork laid out, and this is critical. You've created (part of) a professional image for yourself, made yourself available to the public, and made your product available. Now you need to promote yourself! After this groundwork, now you're at the starting line!

Since the idea of this book is usefulness to the independent musician, we're going to go over a long list of practical ways to promote your music. Each tactic will have a description and some external links where necessary. Here we go. Let's jump in.

Search engine optimization

People typically arrive at websites in three ways: through the use of search engines, clicking links from other websites, or simply by typing in the website address. Even though search engines alone will not complete your promotional arsenal, they will be important.

One thing to make sure of is that in the title tag of your webpage is the name of your band or the keyword you would like to be found with. The title tag is similar to the title of a book. It has to say who you are and get people interested as well. The title tag is used by almost every search engine that uses spiders to crawl your website. It's also the most effective Meta Tag and is used for conveying the theme of your website to the search engines.

For example <title>The Anarchist Cowboys – American punk rock</title>

Here you've listed the name of your band clearly (The Anarchist Cowboys), and you've specified the style or description so people searching the term "American punk" or "punk rock" are more likely to find you. Your influences or an original phrase can also be added to the description. Just keep it concise. A full html example is below:

<head>
<title>Title of Your Webpage Here</title> (bolded for emphasis)
<meta name="description" content="Brief description of the contents of the page">
<meta name="keywords" content="keyword phrases that describe your webpage">
</head>

The main search engines you will need to be listed on are:

1) Google (www.google.com/addurl/?continue=/addurl)
2) Yahoo (http://search.yahoo.com/info/submit.html)
3) MSN (http://search.msn.com/docs/submit.aspx?FORM=WSDD2)

These sites generate the results for all the primary search engines. Dmoz (www.dmoz.org/add.html) feeds thousands of smaller search engines so be sure to sign up there too.

Don't waste your money on services promising to provide submissions to thousands of search engines. We've tried those and they don't help much.

Things that will attract search engine traffic include a site index, footers, and XML feeds. Frames repel them. This is another reason to either go with a service like HostBaby or Bandzoogle. They will help you create a simple, search engine friendly website.

Hiring a webmaster is a great option. Like we said before though, just tell them you don't need all the bells and whistles (flash is not necessary! It will hurt you more than it will help you). You want a website that's simple and will attract people. The last thing you want is your new potential fan being bombarded with unasked for music and digital chaos when clicking on your site link.

Choose effective and clear keywords. (Free music, metal band, heavy metal music, etc) Be sure to mention these terms on your site to strengthen them. Don't go crazy with irrelevant choices either (Kim Kardashian photos, Disney movie clips, Paris Hilton, etc). There are many books dedicated solely to the topic of search engine optimization. "Search Engine Optimization for Dummies" by Peter Kent is a good one. Information found online or via these books can be a big help, but for now, as long as we choose the proper keywords, label our site correctly, and submit to the proper search engines we should be off to a good start.

To find out how to improve your Google page ranking, go to www.google.com/support.

Link Exchanges

Link exchanges can easily become a core part of your online marketing strategy. The more places you are on the web, the easier it is for people to find you, or 'stumble across' you.

Make it easy for others to link to you.

Have a page that displays a variety of different banners that webmasters can place on their sites. Give them the option to place ready-to-paste html in their pages. This can add some incentive, as it is much quicker to cut and paste code.

So who do you want to exchange links with? Well, try going to Google's top lists (http://www.google.com/Top/ or Alexa.com and search for the best by category. Let's explore this a bit more because it's important.

So if you are an industrial band, you want to go to
http://www.google.com/Top/Arts/Music/Styles/R/Rock/Industrial/

See how many of these sites you can exchange links with and/or gain coverage on (we'll go over that later). Next, look in the other categories related to your niche such as
http://www.google.com/Top/Arts/Music/Styles/R/Rock/Industrial/Bands_and_Artists/

http://www.google.com/Top/Arts/Music/Styles/R/Rock/Industrial/Radio/

and

http://www.google.com/Top/Arts/Music/Styles/R/Rock/Industrial/Personal_Pages/

Have some rock in your sound too? Great. Then there are more options. Explore the rock category and send out those emails requesting link exchanges! Sure, this may not sound like much fun but it will be rewarding when you see your website traffic skyrocket. Websites with a higher Google ranking will help your own site ranking improve. Therefore, you should try to exchange links with as many high-ranking websites as possible.

Of course, you also want to offer links to radio shows or podcasts that play your music and websites or magazines that review your music. This is part of being at the bargaining table and having something to offer them. Build those relationships! More on that later.

Independent Music Promotions

Press releases

In the music business, the press release (or news release) is one of the most common tools used to bring an artist free publicity. It's a great way to let people know about your new CD, a tour, free downloads you are offering (keep this in mind – it will get you hits to your site), a label signing, or anything newsworthy that your band is doing. The more newsworthy your press release is the more exposure you will get.

Format is just as important as your content. A poor presentation, or typos, show a lack of professionalism and drastically reduces your chances the release will run as written, or at all for that matter. If submitting the press release by email, make sure to copy it into the body of the message rather than include it as an attachment. Attachments are a big no-no in the industry when you haven't yet built a rapport. Also, not everyone uses the same programs to view these documents.

What is a press release?

Basically, a press release is a simple sheet that provides news and information to editors, dj's, reporters, music fans and individuals in the press. The main thing to keep in mind is it has to be newsworthy. Make sure it reads like a **news release** rather than an **advertisement**. What's your angle? Don't worry – there are LOTS of them.

If your band donates funds from merchandise or CD sales to Amnesty International, for example, human rights organizations may be interested in distributing your news and even discussing your music with you. This could lead to interviews and more press coverage, but we're getting off track here. If your band covered a classic Metallica song, well you'd better make sure your press release gets out to all the Metallica fan forums and that you contact all the fan sites and blogs for coverage. Make sure to include your press release in the email.

Maybe one of the songs on your album is about something controversial. Do you praise or insult a public figure? Maybe one of your songs is a simple homage to small town America.

There is a market for everything.

What your music is about will determine the audience who is interested in it.

Every style has its own distributors. In general, you may want to pay a bit for Billboard's specialized service at www.billboardpublicitywire.com in order to spread your press release. This is a good option for all genres. If you are a metal or heavy rock band, it's a good idea to submit your press releases to www.blabbermouth.net, for example, because they are highly influential.

Once they accept it and you search your press release on Google, you'll notice within the week that many other metal and similar websites have posted your release as well. If this isn't actionable for you, simply insert your style and go to it!

Learn to use Google to your advantage.

It's amazing how many bands don't investigate the leading media, or 'voices', in their genre. Google your style along with the word 'news' and see what comes up. Start a Microsoft Excel document (or Notepad if you don't have it) and list all the relevant websites that report rock music news, country news, hip hop news, or whatever. This is your starting point. Want another trick? Try searching the term **"submit news"** (in quotes) along with "rock music" (or your chosen style). You will find tons of results leading you directly to news submission pages. You can also try terms such as **"Send your news here"** and **"Send news tip"**. Keep making slight changes to both the style description and the news submission term and you will get new results. Add the relevant ones to your document as you go. Don't forget to send that news release as well.

This is how you start learning shortcuts and *work smarter, not harder.* As in martial arts, so with music!

So how do you write a press release?

Start it off with this:

"FOR IMMEDIATE RELEASE" (or FOR RELEASE JULY 1, 2010) and

"For more information, contact:"

Then you need to include your contact information. (It must be a proper number. What if the press wants to call you and offer you an interview?)

Then write your headline. The headline is the only part of the release that should be in capitals. It also must be interesting so people pay attention and decide to bother reading your release and potentially check out your band. Don't be scared of controversy. "LOUISIANA ROCK BAND SLAMS OBAMA" looks more eye-catching than "LOUISIANA ROCK BAND SPEAKS THEIR MINDS". Why?

Well, because unfortunately not many people care if you speak your mind or not. Everyone speaks his or her mind all the time. People are just interested in getting their own two cents in. It's a sad truth. That being said, if you speak your mind on something THEY care about, you can bet they'll be checking the press release with a fine tooth comb! "What did they say about Obama?

Independent Music Promotions

Who are these guys?" Now we're not suggesting that you insult Barack Obama of course. This is just an example.

After the headline, you need to write the body of your press release. This will include the simple details of your story. The first paragraph should grab the reader's interest and clearly explain the headline. Make sure you share what the news is and present it in a 3rd person style (he, she, the band, etc). Do not make the language overly promotional! For example, don't say "The Filthy Speed Demons, currently the best thrash metal band in the world, recently finished their new CD "All Hail the Filthy Speed Demons", which is sure to climb the charts rapidly." Be more objective!

Make sure it's proper and complete because many publications will run your press release verbatim. You can add quotes to make the release more interesting. This is a great idea to insert a comment on your new album or your latest benefit show.

Throw in potent keywords when relevant. Don't just add Angelina Jolie's name to your release if she has nothing to do with your music. However, if you wrote a song about Angelina, you may be on your way to a healthy amount of news coverage.

At the end of the release, summarize your story and add any "About Us" information that you think is necessary. "More information on the Filthy Speed Demons can be found at www.filthyspeeddemons.com." Finish it up with a contact for further information.

End your press release with the symbol "###" (without the quotation marks) after your last lines of text. This lets the editor know they have successfully received the entire release. It's really that simple.

FOR IMMEDIATE RELEASE

For more information, contact:

Your Name
Your Street Address
City, State, Zip Code
Phone
Fax
Email

HEADLINE

MONTH DAY#, YEAR (CITY, STATE) – This is the who, what, where, when, and why. Make sure the first paragraph summarizes your news clearly.

Add additional details here.

About The Band: (additional information)

For further information, contact Your Name at (xxx) xxx-xxxx.

###

So now you've got your press release done. We mentioned some ways to distribute your release. Put some time into your research. It will be worth it. You basically want it to show up in as many places as possible. Don't underestimate the power of a strong press release.

Another thing we've been hinting at but haven't talked about in depth – Build relationships! Keep tabs on who posted your release and create a document for yourself with the emails and websites who helped you. Call it your "list of allies" or something similar. You'll be surprised how fast it grows if you thank those people and publications.

In many cases, simply sending an email to thank a particular website or magazine for publishing your release can have a dual purpose. You can thank them for "supporting you in the past" and publishing your news releases, and ask for an interview or a CD review to "further the relationship". Be sure to say something like "Please let me know anything you need" and be ready to post banners and links, provide high quality photos and bio information – anything they need. Also, when you approach publications with your press release, don't spam them! Contact them individually by introducing yourself and possibly commenting on their writing or their publication. Let them know you're a real person. Remember, press releases are part of building relationships and they are part of the bait to generate even more press for your band.

Generate MORE press – GET THOSE REVIEWS

Our strategy of Behind-the-scenes marketing

Well, that's one of the main reasons you bought the book, isn't it? Here's the thing. We've scoured the net and a lot of articles on this topic are missing the mark. Yes, you can choose to hire a PR firm if you have the funds. If you choose to do so, there are good companies who run successful press campaigns for independent artists. Alternatively, if you're willing to work at it, you can certainly generate a ton of press yourself. Let's go through a few methods rarely described elsewhere. In fact, this one in particular is one of our original ideas. Our advice is that you use it right away and count the results.

Be personal and/or stroke the ego.

DON'T ALWAYS GO THROUGH THE MAIN CHANNELS.

That could well be the most important sentence in this book. How do you get ahead in this world? Do you wait in line for everything? How about when the line is 1,000 people long? Some artists take longer than others to realize it but you must, and we'll repeat this often, **BUILD RELATIONSHIPS.**

If someone knows nothing about you and you offer him or her nothing in return, there is about a 1/100 chance they will cover your music. That works fine if you want to send 1,000 emails to get *potentially* 10 reviews and burn a lot of bridges in the meantime.

Being personal means more than just copying and pasting the person's name into your pre-written email template. Of course, the press release or album information part of your email can be pre-written. The rest should be original and engaging. Anyone who runs a podcast, or writes for a music publication, is bombarded by bands on a very regular basis. You have the opportunity to either make someone's day or aggravate them.

Ask yourself what typically makes your day as an independent musician? It could very well be that one email you get from a fan who appreciates your music. Maybe they have a particular favourite song and they tell you why. You think "This person actually listened to me". This is the same feeling you want the independent press to get when they read your emails.

If you write the typical "Check out my band" email, it's the equivalent of people posting their advertisements on your MySpace wall.

What can you do to build the relationship?

What we're trying to say is: If you are a metal band and you go to the Google listing of Top metal websites (http://www.google.com/Top/Arts/Music/Styles/R/Rock/Heavy_Metal/) you may be tempted to immediately go to their contact sections and follow their submission policies verbatim. For some of these websites, that would certainly be the best route.

We're going to go through this in great detail since it's critical and it seems nobody else covers the topic in too much depth.

Sometimes going by the rules doesn't pay. You may submit all of your CD's to a popular publication year after year and never get a review – or any coverage at all. This is when you change your tactic.

The media are not so intimidating. They are just groups of individuals! Therefore, when you can, contact them INDIVIDUALLY. This is how **you get into 'the fortress'**. When we say the fortress, we refer to a popular music website, magazine or publication.

Contact INDIVIDUALS. The media is a lot less scary when we realize that they are all just collectives of individuals. Independent music media is even easier to crack. Many of the reviewers don't get paid much (if at all) and they are music fans like you. How intimidating is that? That means they have something in common with you. Use that to your advantage.

Tactic 1) EMBRACE THE EGO:

Try looking up articles on YOUR favourite bands, or most importantly, bands that are similar in style to your own - and contact the person who wrote the piece. Reviews on niche bands give you something unique to talk about. You can relate to the writer about being one of the few people to discover the band. Even better, congratulate them on discovering the band in question!

Say something personal about the review/article - why you liked it, what you like about the band, etc. Be natural. Ask a question such as "Have you heard such-and-such a band? I think you'd love them." This gets a conversation started. Keep in mind these writers typically get no feedback from their reviews and articles so positive feedback or a pat on the back will get their attention. In the title of the email mention who the email is attention to and how you found them.

For example "Attn Sean – your Queens of the Stone Age review". Guaranteed that will get Sean's attention. It looks much better than "Attn reviews – Please review my band!" Count on those to go to the delete box more often than not.

In the SECOND paragraph, you mention your band. Don't be pushy. Provide a website link, or better yet, have a digital download of your album sent to their email address. (Bandzoogle and HostBaby should have this capability. Use it! It will save you money.)

Here is a template for you to get an idea. Keep in mind the idea is to be honest and actually communicate with this person. Change your wording every time! Try to genuinely relate to the writer.

HEADER: "Attn Sean – Your Queens of the Stone Age review"

BODY: "Hi Sean, This is James from the rock band Broken Jaw Dance Party. I found _____ Magazine through your rather excellent review of Queens of the Stone Age's album "Lullabies to Paralyse". I thought it was well done and agree with your favourite track choices (mine are "Little Sister" and "Burn the Witch" as well). I'm curious as to what you think of their latest release "Era Vulgaris". To me it's a stronger album. Also, have you heard (insert band name here)? Given your musical preferences you may get into them. Check them out and let me know what you think.

I've sent you a digital copy (email the digital copy of the album to Jame's email address. It should arrive as a free download that he can access easily) of Broken Jaw Dance Party's new album "Curbstomp Disco", as I think you'd enjoy it. Queens are a big influence of ours (give a short story of how you got into them, or keep it simple) and a review would be appreciated of course.

Thanks for your time and once again, great job on the review!

Sean

Broken Jaw Dance Party

www.brokenjawdanceparty.com

(include email and phone number contact in signature)

Tactic 2) MAKE A FRIEND:

We encourage you to check out "Staff" sections on music websites. Many music websites will have an area where they provide a list of their staff with email addresses, photos, music preferences, hobbies etc. Find someone you relate to and email these people! Once again – have a conversation first and foremost. Then, on a side note, ask for the coverage in the second paragraph.

Remember: This works for interviews too.

If one of the person's interests is politics, you could say "My band wrote a song about the current financial crisis. Maybe we could do an interview for your publication and discuss this." (Just an example. It may be difficult to write an interesting song about the financial crisis!)

The whole idea is – when you visit a website; think to yourself "Someone who writes for this site will relate to me". Think of it as making a new ally or friend. One thing that's hard for musicians to understand sometimes is that we're all music fans. It's not all about the musician. Bands that simply send out mass emails asking media (and fans for that matter) to "check out our album" do not get nearly the results that bands who express interest in who they are writing to.

Find something you are genuinely interested in about the person's opinions or ideas. If you can't find anything at all, maybe you should go the main route.

Tactic 3) THE NORMAL ROUTE DONE RIGHT:

What is the normal route? The normal route is going to the website or publication's "contact" or "FAQ" section and finding out their submission procedures. Do everything they ask. Then send a quick, polite email to the main email provided introducing yourself and letting them know that your CD is on the way. Thank them for the opportunity and let them know you are keen to get involved with their site and are happy to cross promote as well. Be polite, thankful and helpful!

Make a note of the email, publication, and date of contact in a document such as a Microsoft Excel sheet, and follow up in 4 weeks or so. Many times you will get an individual reply to your first email, so you will have an INDIVIDUAL to follow up with. See how it all comes together?

Remember, you'll need to use more than one tactic to generate reviews. Some larger websites do not display any contact information for their staff. You will have to follow tactic 3 and be vigilant. Follow up!

Remember – The media are the opinion makers.

Finding out about new music through the media can take place through a review, feature, interview, or some sort of radio play or music sharing. If you respect the source, you will be more likely to buy.

So whose opinion is worthwhile? This has expanded rapidly since the Internet has become more and more accessible. There are internet-only publications with readerships in the tens of thousands. You need to get your music to these people. Talk to them. Connect with them. Send your music to places such as Pitchfork Media and PopMatters.

Blogs have become extremely important in recent years. Look up music blogs that cater to your style of music and contact the author in the Behind-the-scenes marketing style. Allow these blogs to share your album if they want to. If the right blog posts your album or talks about your band, it can go **viral**.

For an overwhelming, but hopefully exciting list of music mp3 blogs that can post your music, go to http://hypem.com/list. The way the Hype Machine works is it tracks a huge amount of mp3 and music blogs. If a post contains MP3 links, it adds those links to its database and displays them on the front page of the Hype Machine's website. You can also search similar artists to your band on Hype Machine, and choose to contact those blogs only. This can get you a ton of new listeners.

Does this take much time?

Sure. It will initially. But the results can be shocking. Do you want a press page filled with quotes from music publications raving about your band? That's the way to do it (provided your music is strong, of course). Get personal and you will get those reviews coming in.

Reviews typically come in over a period of 1-6 months as well, which can be a good thing. Writers can tend to be busy people. This can mean that if you connect with enough people, you'll get a few efficient writers who provide you reviews within a few weeks. Remember – you are planting seeds. Don't let yourself get discouraged.

Now you've got your press page off to a good start. Be sure to get their permission before posting the review in full or in part on your website. If you've connected with enough people, you will continue to see reviews coming in over the next long while – people you forgot you contacted will be sending you reviews, and this keeps your band in the spotlight somewhat. Pat yourself on the back every time you get a positive review.

Allow yourself to celebrate because working, as an independent musician, is a series of small victories.

Can you use negative reviews?

Yes and no. If the negative review goes something like "The instrumentation was subpar and the vocals were awkwardly bad. I felt embarrassed listening to this band. Boy, do they ever suck." then you probably would not want to post it on your website. It's bad enough that it's posted anywhere!

But if the review goes something like "Where do these punks get off saying these terrible things about the government? The music was pure noise! It's immoral, un-American, and I don't know how people could listen to this musical chaos!"....And let's say you are an anarchist punk band or a politically charged heavy metal group, it's fair game and would work for you rather than against you. Get the idea?

Why do we call this Behind-the-Scenes Marketing?

Now we've gone over some clear examples of what we call behind-the-scenes marketing for independent bands. The reason we call it behind-the-scenes marketing is because the viewing audience, the music fans, **do not** get access to your personalized emails or an unimpressive image of your lead singer sitting in front of a computer emailing away.

What the viewing audience will see is a "critically acclaimed" new band. It's that simple. Make friends who will "create the frontline" for you. You don't do it yourself. As we've said, if you call yourself "the next Nirvana", people will laugh. But if Revolver Magazine makes this claim about your band, you may just find that people rush to your website to hear your new album.

Newsletters and Mailing Lists

A necessity for your website is to have a visible mailing list or newsletter sign up. If all the people visiting your website simply come and go, what good is it to you? You will want to capture their name and email address. Your band mailing list should quickly become one of your best marketing tools. Both Bandzoogle and HostBaby will give you mailing list capability.

If you hire a webmaster, they can create one for you, or alternatively you can sign up for an outside service such as www.aweber.com, who will manage an email list for you.

Newsletters, used effectively, are one of the best promotional tools a band can have, and they're free. Make sure you are collecting names and email addresses at your live shows and events as well. Cover all fronts. If you are collecting emails through your website, your facebook, your MySpace, and your live shows, you'll have thousands of fans on your mailing list in no time.

So what should be in your newsletter?

Well, that's up to you but there are guidelines that can help. It's a good idea to have an intro or even a table of contents in order to let people know what's coming. As far as content goes, there's the obvious –

1) News articles (possibly your latest press release)
2) Recent reviews (which you're overflowing with after following the steps in our reviews chapter, right?)
3) Interesting information about members of the band (you ARE interesting, aren't you?)
4) Fan comments (Quotes from fan feedback – for example "Thanks for the CD guys! Every song is amazing and it's been in my CD player all month!" – Sarah from Los Angeles)
5) Contests (We'll get more into the significance of contests later, but it's a great way to get people used to paying more attention to your mailing list)
6) Upcoming events (What's coming down the pipe?)
7) Something personal (This is optional. Possibly include a recent blog. People get turned off if your whole newsletter is sales based. Talk to them. Give them something original to read.)
8) Humour (Put it all together with humour. Don't be boring. Don't just give a sales pitch. Be a human being!)
9) Recognition for your allies (Post links to "friends of the band". This could be radio or podcasts who have played your music recently or a website that has covered your band. It's a way of saying thanks and getting more exposure for them. They will appreciate it.)
10) Your merchandise (What are you selling? You want to sell, don't you? Entice people to buy.)

11) Questions! You can ask your fans for feedback. What songs would they like to see you cover? What town would they like you to visit next? What song should you promote to radio next?
12) Unsubscribe information (Let people know they are not obligated to receive the newsletter.)

Does that give you some good ideas? Make sure you run a spell check. If you miss out on this some people will think you're unprofessional and cancel their subscription.

How do you build your mailing list?

There are many ways to build your mailing list. Here are a few ideas.

Advertise it on your homepage and your social networks.

Create an incentive. Have a contest. "Sign up for our mailing list and get a free mp3 download of our new single" or "Sign up for our mailing list and get entered into our ultimate prize pack contest". This could be a CD, poster and t-shirt, for example. Be creative. Send a lock of your bassist's hair. It's all up to you.

Collect email addresses at your live performances, as we mentioned earlier. Have a mailing list at your merchandise table and make sure you get an email address from anyone who buys a CD or compliments the band.

Get everyone in the band involved in building the list. Have each member gather email addresses from their co-workers, friends and family. It's important for the morale of the band to not let any member slack off. By promoting yourself, you're feeding the energy and excitement of your band. The more results you get, the more motivation you will have to move forward and see what's around the corner. Advertise your mailing list on your personal facebook. When you run into an acquaintance, ask for their email to include. Be aggressive.

Viral Marketing

Why bother going viral?

Advertising on the internet (through banner ads, pay-per-click, pop-up windows, and other ad marketing) has been producing worse and worse results. At this point it's barely worth it for even large companies to go these routes. If you had a choice when watching television to sit through the advertisements or just watch the show's content, what would you choose? When watching television, you have to go by the rules, but on the internet, the user has control – ***and they absolutely do not want to see advertising***. Marketers are spending more and more on traditional advertising methods to achieve a fraction of the result.

This does not necessarily mean that people have completely rejected the messages of marketing or advertising campaigns. After all, we all still buy products. It's simply the WAY that marketing products that has changed.

Most people prefer looking up specific things online – get what they want specifically and go. People will typically ignore anything that looks like advertising. Advertising may work in the physical world but not so much in the online world.

What's the solution? It's simple. Stop marketing AT people. Somehow, we need to get people marketing to each other. And when we do market, we need to be human about it. Make it engaging. Advertise through other people's words and mouths as opposed to your own. For example, product promotion has moved mainly to places such as word-of-mouth and social networks. People who frequent and contribute to these networks and websites act like advertisers in a lot of ways. They:

- Spread the word about new products or services.
- Communicate the incentives, features and potential benefits.
- Display a respected opinion and create peer pressure to follow suit.
- E-mail the URL to friends and acquaintances.
- Advertise the product in their 'favorites' lists, blog, or by posting traditional banners.

They are advertisers though they are most often unaware of it and normally do not get paid for it. Yet they are much more effective than most expensive marketing campaigns because they are on the inside track. They are at the heart of things.

On social and word-of-mouth networks, people feel comfortable discussing their favorite products because they don't feel targeted or exploiter by companies. As far as they are concerned, they are empowered. In their minds, they are making their own choices as a consumer. They have the power. Because of this, they promote more whole-heartedly the products they feel passionately about.

Sounds great, doesn't it?

In the tradition of this book following a no-nonsense, actionable approach, let's start with a list of viral marketing ideas for the independent musician.

Think of your CD as a virus.

That's right. **Your CD is a virus.** And there are roughly 6.75 billion potential carriers of this virus. With more and more competition vying for the hearts and minds of the buying public, it's getting more and more difficult to penetrate the market. You need to find the people who are going to be good spreaders of your virus and pass it on with ease to others. This could be the media or it could be personal bloggers – people who use social networks. Treat them well and give out creative incentives liberally.

Every time your band name gets mentioned or your CD gets reviewed, think of your virus getting stronger. **The more of a push you give it, the stronger it gets and the more viral it becomes.**

The people who will spread your virus the most are the people who others trust. Some of these people are the music authorities – the bloggers, the podcasters, the radio hosts, the reviewers. Let the music authorities spread your virus!

Ask yourself, "What can I do to make my product more like a virus?" Have you thought about the context of your music? Sure, your songs have intense meanings. How can you spread those meanings? Is there anything that would engage the general public? Relate to them? Aggravate them? Amuse them? Upset them? Inspire them to respond or share an opinion of their own?

What if you posted relevant videos all over the internet related to your songs – possibly something timely or controversial. Something political? Something hilarious? We'll get to that.

Take over one location first.

If you're going to war or playing RISK, you don't send small amounts of troops to every country and hope things turn out for the best. You build a strong base and spread it in a way that no one has the strength to beat you.

One way to try to go viral is to take over one location to start. Pick a forum, a website, a social network, or hey, a country. Why not? Ever hear of artists getting big in Japan or Germany? It could work as a fun experiment, and has worked for many bands. Simply focus in particular on your country of choice on social networks. Look up the music websites and zines for that country and get involved. You'd be surprised.

Many countries have large populations eager to hear new and original music. You may find that the North American crowd can tend to be cynical and close-minded to your marketing at times. Focus on another country and let them spread your music and message! This translates and spreads elsewhere.

On a smaller level, if you choose a website and get a good review, obviously you have had conversations with and befriended the reviewer if you've followed the behind-the-scenes marketing strategy. Here are some other ways to dominate the website and community associated with it.

Use the leverage from your review to score an interview and also a featured band spot.

Send your news releases regularly so the website is consistently reporting on your band. Make sure it's relevant.

Send free digital or physical copies to the rest of the staff, thanking them for the support of your band.

Show up on the forums with your website in your signature.

Comment on their blogs and reviews. Be relevant and positive.

Reach out to their readership when possible.

Talk to people and encourage them to spread the virus.

If you wanted to get popular in school you would find out who the cool kids are and befriend them. If you want to get popular on a social network, look up the top personal users. Contact them and introduce them to your music. Befriend them. Take an interest in them. Create reasons why they should spread your music. Use incentives when needed. Reward the people who are on your side.

Use what works on you!

When you scour a music website or magazine looking for a new band to add to your iPod playlist or CD collection, only a select few will stand out to you. Why is that? Is it their artwork? The promotional language used to describe the band? The reviews listed? Maybe the band photo?

Rearrange your own press materials and advertising if necessary to emulate (within reason) what looks effective to you. You will be marketing to people who relate to you, remember.

Are you ready to make your product a virus?

Make sure you've prepared the necessary elements to go viral. Your website, music and content must be intact and impressive. Your product must be interesting! Ask yourself objectively "Would I spread this around? Would I tell my friends about this?" If the honest answer is no, don't panic. This just means there is still room for more creativity and experimentation.

Use your current allies.

Make a list of everyone who is on your side. Keep track of their names, roles (family, radio dj, blogger, fan, etc), and email addresses on a document such as Microsoft Excel or a custom program. Keep them in the loop at to what's new with your band and how they can help you. Make it worthwhile and treat them well. Whenever you get played by a new radio show or get covered by a new website, add them to your list of allies. Once again, use cross-promotion, incentives and thank yous to keep them on your allies list.

Multiply your allies.

Yes indeed. Ask your current allies if they know anyone else you can contact for airplay or press. You may be surprised what comes up. Ask if you can tell this new person that you were referred by them. They will usually be delighted to give you a few names.

Plus, approaching someone new saying "John Smith highly recommended your radio show for our band and suggested that I get in touch with you. John recently interviewed us at his Rock Star Nation website. Would you be interested in a review or interview?" gives you a much better chance of getting coverage than approaching on your own. By helping you, they see themselves doing a favor or coming through for a friend. Their ego is stroked just by knowing that someone recommended them. Most people will want to come through in this type of scenario.

Make your marketing plan your own social network. Multiply your allies to build your army. Pretty soon you will have enough press to rival a major label act. It's all about image.

Randomly reward people.

Word-of-mouth is not always created by set-in-stone freebies and campaigns. What does this mean to you? Well, it's a very good idea to randomly reward people.

Go above and beyond.

If a new person signs up for your street team, mailing list, or buys your CD, why not send them a personal email letting them know you've sent them digital copies of 2 of your albums to say thanks. Most people would be thrilled to be contacted personally by a member of the band, and on top of that be given free stuff, they would surely tell a few friends. Be generous on a person-to-person basis and you'll be surprised at the word-of-mouth this can generate about your band.

Don't worry about profit quite yet.

You've got to launch this thing in a big way before you focus specifically on profit. The CD orders will eventually become a positive by-product of your viral campaign. Be very generous. Create reasons for your band to have an inside circle. Does your website allow people to log in? Are there member benefits such as extra free downloads? Are you providing a good incentive for those fans who are signing up for your mailing list or E-team? When someone does buy your CD, are you giving them something else as well such as a digital copy of your previous album or a previously unreleased track?

If it's digital, it doesn't cost anything. One common mistake that independent bands and musicians make in this day and age is being overly stingy and paranoid about their music. Here's a tip: If your band records a CD, sets up a website with 30 second previews of each track and waits for the fans to come swooping in, it's simply not going to happen.

Bands spend a lot of time asking "Should we offer this track for free? Will that be too much? But we won't make any money!" ***This is the indie band's paranoia.***

Remember that a digital product is infinite. When someone downloads your song, you have a new listener. Period. Yes, they may have downloaded it for free, but you have no less stock. Now that we are beyond dealing with physical products, you don't have to worry quite as much about running out of product and potentially giving away too much stock for promotional purposes.

Beyond that, you should actively be looking for potential virus carriers to send free music to! Tell them all you'd like in return is that they post it somewhere or send it to someone else. Tell them to treat your music as a virus. They will most likely get a kick out of the idea and be appreciative of your modern attitude. It's this attitude that is going to get your music spread. Don't waste time on the old school way of thinking – if you do that you may as well be a record label going out of business.

Another way to think of it is:

The more places you are, the more places people can find you.

So it's simple. Get in more places! These days, it's not just the media that are turning people on to new music. It's the music fans, thanks to the help of social networking. Get your music into as many receptive hands as possible and encourage them to spread it themselves. Get into more places.

People will download music for free – no matter what.

You need to accept this. The record labels have not. Many artists have not. People will download music for free whether you offer your own music for free or not. Would you rather them have your music and potentially spread it or not? In fact, you not only need to accept the fact that people want free music. You need to embrace it and make it a core part of your promotional strategy.

The more music you have distributed for you free of charge, the more you will sell. Some of the people who catch the virus will be the ones who prefer to support the artist by paying for music. Just remember, right or wrong, it's the nature of the business today that music is essentially free. The only people who pay for music are those who:

1) *Prefer to support the artist and have the funds to do so*
2) *Good Samaritans or people who feel it is wrong to download music for free*
3) *Do not have the means (such as a computer or file-sharing network) to download for free*
4) *Do not have the technical know-how to download for free*

Sound blunt? Well, somebody's got to be honest! It's only when we stop beating our heads against the wall that we can try a new tactic.

Word of mouth has changed. This is an important thing to remember. Word of mouth has changed. And you can use this knowledge in your favor. Twenty years ago, if I loved a new band I would tell a few friends and maybe make a mix tape. Today, if someone gets into a new band, they may add the band name to their MySpace Music preferences, join the band's fan club on Facebook (typically all their friends will see this), add the band to their Last.fm playlist, mention the band in their favorite forum, and write about the band in their personal blog if they have one. Word of mouth is happening online in blogs, social media and forums. The bands who understand this are the ones that get known.

A recommendation that would have died within a small friend circle previously now lasts forever on the internet. Use this to your advantage.

Don't underestimate the average Joe! It could be the biggest mistake you ever make. This is another reason to be generous with your music.

Have a "Send this page to a friend" option on every page of your website.

This is something that will put you "ahead of the curve", and it's something very few independent musicians do. Give people multiple ways to spread your music around. This is one of the best ways. If bloggers do it, and news websites do it, why can't you? All it takes is an html code, and you can look these up quite easily using Google search. If someone really enjoys one of your songs or blogs, this gives them an opportunity to send the link to their friends immediately. Statistics show that these options work, and without them, people simply would not go to the effort in most cases to refer. You will need a free script to download to add this feature to your site. For a good one: Click here

Get on YouTube. This can be in the form of a professional video (It's not as difficult as you think. Hire a film student do shoot your video for you. It will cost a fraction of the price of a professional director and should produce some good results) or simply amateur footage of one of your live performances.

You can show a slideshow of your band photos and post a song from your latest CD. It can be invaluable to become familiar with YouTube as an independent artist. Use stock footage, footage of political figures or current events, something artistic or eye-catching – anything that represents the mood of your music or will potentially get people talking, and more importantly, spreading your virus. You can use relevant keywords to attract people to your video. Many bands have gained thousands of new fans by simply posting a slideshow or video on YouTube. Is there a new movie coming out that has gained a lot of buzz? Post clips of the movie set to one of your best songs. As the recent Alice in Wonderland movie approached, many bands took this opportunity and set their own music to clips of the upcoming film. This resulted in thousands upon thousands of listens, and many new fans. Make sure to build those relationships as well. Comment other similar sounding bands and music outlets. Sign up for their channels and favorite their videos. Build your network.

Get creative!

If it's controversial or current in some way, that is even better. For example, there is a live video on YouTube of a performance by the Dillinger Escape Plan where the singer runs into the crowd frantically, stepping on their shoulders, screaming his head off, the whole bit. People started spreading this video virally and it helped spread the word about the band.

The point is, if people like your video and your music they will tell their friends about it. In lieu of having a professionally done music video, there are plenty of things you can do to gain thousands of new fans online.

To create your music videos from slideshows and video clips combined you can use free software programs like Windows Movie Maker, for example. If you want something more professional and you are ok with spending some money you can always try:

- Adobe Premiere Elements 4.0
- Power Director 6
- Vegas Movie Studio 8

Set up your own channel on YouTube.

Having your own channel is a great way of attracting people to your music, and for creating a thriving community. Within your YouTube channel you can add your favorite videos by others. When those videos are viewed, your channel is visible which means that YouTube users are able to click through and find out what else your channel has to offer. This is a perfect reason to expand your content.

Think about the kinds of things your fans love to watch and save them to your YouTube channel. It's a great way to bring people into contact with your music.

Have a "Send this page to a friend" option on every page of your website.

This is a critical move towards going viral. You must give people a smooth way to spread your website around. There are html codes that can easily be integrated with any website for this purpose.

Spread your banner on social networks such as MySpace. Make your banner and banner code available. Create an incentive (see a theme here?) for people to post it on their own profiles. You could offer the first 10 people to add your banner (or song, for that matter!) to their MySpace profile a spot on your Top Friends list. Once that's done, start a different contest.

In order to add a banner to your site that shows people a code they can easily post on their own websites, here is a template:

```
<br><br>

<img src="YOUR IMAGE " border="0">

<br>COPY / PASTE<br>the code below to your site to link to our band!<br><textarea name="textarea" cols="70" rows="3">

<a href="YOUR WEBSITE "><img src="YOUR IMAGE " border="0" /></a><br />

</textarea>

<br><br>
```

Just copy and paste the above code into your website. This will allow people to spread the word for you by posting the banner themselves.

Create an E-Card. Have an E-Card created for your band. E-Cards are a perfect example of viral marketing. The idea is for people to forward them to each other. Start it off with your family if you have to! They're the most proud of you! They may have people on their email lists who will forward it on for you.

Send your music to podcasts and internet radio shows. We'll go over specifics about these two later, but the spreading of your music to new listeners through these formats is a form of viral marketing.

Create a downloadable screensaver.

Make a simple screensaver that has your website address and band name in bold letters. Design a particularly artistic screensaver and people will be more inclined to keep it. You can download simple to use software at www.download.com

Be controversial or compelling. We talked about this earlier. Remember the press release reference to the "Louisiana rock band slams Obama"? Well, how about posting a YouTube video with his photo? How about an e-card that people can spread virally? Only do this if it suits your music. No matter what your subject matter, there should be a viral market for you.

How to Sell

A big question often asked in today's music market is how independent musicians can sell product. After all, most people steal their music these days, right? Well, not exactly. There are still ways to make money at this thing called music. We'll go over a wide range of tips.

Create abundance in your mind: A lot of musicians have unhealthy attitudes towards money. Many musicians tell themselves that money is unimportant, and that only other things in life, such as "love", are. If you want to be a successful musician, you will need to discard this idea right away. Call it "punk rock ethic". Call it whatever you like. Chances are you're broke.

Change your attitude: There is a lot of doom and gloom in musician's minds these days. Don't even hang around with these people, let alone allow yourself to be one. Music should be played for the love of it before all else. Don't let anyone convince you that your art is not welcome in this world. Be a positive force.

Target the market with buzz: We talked about "creating the frontline". This may take a few months, but once it's complete, your band looks much more appealing to the buyer. Go to www.myspace.com/extralifetheband and check out their Media section. This is a perfect example of press quotes, and you can certainly take it further. We would encourage it in fact! But that's not all buzz is about.

Heavily promote yourself on Facebook as well as other social networks. Get that airplay. Think of more and more incentives for people to spread your music. This will result in more CD sales.

Go viral: Get people posting your mp3's all over the place (the ones you want distributed, anyway). Persuade people to write about you in their blogs and forum posts. Put up YouTube videos featuring your songs. Spread the message.

Talk to people: Be a real person. Talk to people on Facebook. Comment their profiles. Participate on forum chats. ALWAYS leave your web address as your signature. Many people are more likely to buy your CD if they feel they have had a good conversation with you or that they 'know someone in the band'. It's a win-win situation.

Music consultants will tell you that at the independent level, bands and band members must be accessible.

Create profiles for each of your band members and make them accessible. Provide contact information for each member on your official website. Some people may have questions for the lyricist about the meaning of a particular song. Other people may want to ask the guitarist about his gear, or how he or she got started. Once they get that friendly response directly from the member of the band it will get them on board. They will be a loyal fan and much more likely to buy a CD.

Social Networks

So how should you run your Facebook, MySpace or Reverbnation profile? Let's start with what you should put on your profile and what you shouldn't.

An eye-catching photo: Make sure you have at least one professional band photo or a slick looking band logo to put as your profile picture. This is what will show up on the searches and other people's friend lists. Many people will send you an add request or a "like" simply because your photo is interesting.

Your music: Showcase your music. Make sure there is at least one free download. Mention this in your blog. You don't just want your music on your social network profiles and your official website. You want your music on people's iPods, as well as their social and personal play lists. Free downloads can get you spreading quickly.

Another tip is to hold off on the auto play setting. People are more likely to check out your music and stay on your site if it doesn't start blaring away at them when they have other websites open.

A short bio: Be very brief. This can even be shorter than the full-length bio you created for your official website. Get to the point. This leaves more room for accolades and press clippings.

Press: Many advisors don't mention this but we highly recommend it. Put your press quotes in the same area as your bio. It could look something like this:

"Aggressive guitars, Cut-throat vocals, and top-notch production. One of the best releases of 2009."

— Rock Star Magazine

"This band is certainly on the verge. Keep your ears peeled."

— The Daily Revue

"Dense and complex…musical mayhem delivered in spades."

— Metal Madness

…And so on. Remember, you are presenting an image. Before you decide to see a movie, do you check the reviews? Many people do. A common practise is for people to check a site such as www.rottentomatoes.com before deciding to spend their money on a movie. It's the same thing with CD purchases. The more reviews and 4 or 5 star ratings you have, the more curious people are about you. You appear to be a critically acclaimed band as opposed to simply a band. And it will be the truth, of course. This is how you build yourself.

Your website address: Get all those interested people to your homepage! It's unprofessional for a band to only have a MySpace profile. You have a head office, right?

Links to your stuff

If you have merchandise, music online or a physical CD to sell, make sure you have clear links for people to buy them. If they are on your website, you have their attention. Now you need to make it seamless for them to purchase your creations.

Additional photos and video: Content is key. For those people who want to check out your attractive bassist (It's shallow, but you'd be surprised) then let them get to it. Have more professional photos in your photos section. Have live videos available on your social network sites as well. Post your YouTube video!

Background images: Only add a background image to your website if it looks really slick. There are codes you can get online for creating a background from any image. The main thing is visibility. Your social profiles must be easy to read and follow.

Comments: Do you want people to comment your profile? YES! Do you want SPAM comments? NO! Set up your comments wall so that you have to approve all comments. Do not approve anything except for comments related specifically to the band. Comments posting videos, large posters, or "Thanks for the add" will hurt your image.

Don't think you're being impolite by declining these comments. They are the ones spamming. If you take the effort to say something individual then they should too. The comments you want to ACCEPT are more like "Great sound guys! Come to my city and play live!" or "I love your song _____. You guys are amazing!" Get the idea?

Should you build your friend lists? Of course you should. Just make sure it's targeted. It won't do you much good to be friends with a bunch of spammers. Search for music fans who are into the same bands that you sound like and send your requests that way. You can download a friend-adding program to help you out, but don't go overboard! It's better to have 2,000 quality friends who you can keep in better contact with and use as a network to work with than having 20,000 friends who could not care less about your music.

Blog

Regularly add new blogs and information. Just be sure to give them an interesting headline because that's all that will display on your actual profile. People will need to click on the link to see the blog. So make it interesting!

Steal your way to the top

One of the best ways to get ahead on social networks is to steal tactics. Find bands that are similar to yours but more successful. Start connecting with their fans. Add them as friends with a personal message. Post comments on their page – the less spammy and the more personal, the better.

Be everyone's BFF

Top friends are important. The more people who count you as a top friend, the more visible you become. Run a trial. Contact people and give them a copy of your album or a free download if they make you a top friend. Create an incentive for people to advertise your band in this way. Find a way to help them in return.

Reply!

It's amazing how many bands get lazy and don't respond to their messages. By responding personally to messages you are building a personal connection with your fans. You are taking a big step on the path to making them a true fan.

This is just the beginning. With social networking you can do as little or as much as you want to make it work for you. Just remember – the more real friends you have, the more plays your songs have, the more comments you have, the more you are interacting with your fans, the more successful you are going to be.

Social Networking and Opportunity Websites

As an independent musician, you should create a presence on as many of these websites as possible. Use all of their tools to your advantage:

Reverbnation – Like MySpace once was, Reverbnation is a huge community with numerable services for independent artists. Definitely sign up and make your profile as complete as possible. Whether you pay extra for the enhanced memberships is up to you. Try it out fully and see if it's worth it to your band.

Music XRay – With Sonicbids and Reverbnation becoming so crowded, it's good to have a fresh, new face on the block. Music XRay allows independent musicians to submit their music for potential licensing in film, television, video games, label roster consideration, radio play, or for review in magazines and blogs.

MySpace – It once was the ultimate social network for musicians, and now only a shadow of its former self. In today's music market many are suggesting that bands do away with the MySpace profile and stick to Reverbnation, Facebook, Twitter and an official website.

Flickr – Flickr is a very popular photo sharing social network. Post photos of your fans, the audience at your shows, your tour photos, you at music festivals. Get your fans involved in your band through your photography. This site can become a very effective marketing tool. The search results on Flickr are different and much more extensive in many cases than Google. Encourage your fans to send photos of the band (or themselves at one of your shows) to add to your Flickr page.

Facebook – networking and social network. Set up a group and a fan club for your band. Make sure all the members of your band advertise your music and website through their personal Facebook profiles. Add links and videos to existing Facebook music groups. Join any and all groups relevant to your style. Have your friends do the same.

Encourage them to respond to your posts and promote you. Don't hide your identity. Be accessible.

With 70 million users, the opportunity Facebook offers is almost unmatched. They are always expanding their promotional services. For example, fans can now add promotional badges to their personal Facebook sites to let others know they love your band. Get your friends to spread the word. Facebook also offers targeted pay-per-click advertising. This means that, for example, you can create an ad for your band that targets only people from Vancouver, BC who are fans of the rock band Tool. Consistent advertising within your niche could be a very valuable investment for your band. What is $100 per month between 4 or 5 band members? It could mean 100 new fans. This can be useful in your promotion strategy.

Last.fm has a great Facebook application to share your play lists (which should, of course, feature your own music). iLike is another Facebook music application that lets Facebook users go directly to iTunes to make music purchases.

Also, **Wildfire**, the number one application for sweepstakes and contests, is fully integrated with Facebook and designed to help bands go viral. If you hold a sweepstakes, make sure the prize has some cash or a gift card along with your band swag. This will allow you to sneak your contest into multiple categories on the popular sweepstakes websites and get thousands more entries. You can find more information on Wildfire at www.wildfireapp.com.

Google Reader – RSS feed aggregator (Learn about RSS. It could become the most important aspect of your website.)

Tumblr – scrapbook blogs, or 'tumblelogs'

Wikipedia - all of human knowledge in editable form. Add your information only when relevant. If you are a young band, keep the item to the point. Include links to online articles referencing you so the information can be easily verified. Do not add yourself until you have set up a strong presence, have played live extensively, and have garnered a high amount of press and reviews. Wikipedia tends to delete bands who they consider to be irrelevant.

Del.icio.us - social book marking

YouTube - video sharing. You should be using this tool right away. This can be a much better tool than Reverbnation and Facebook combined, when used properly. One idea that bands often disregard on YouTube is advertising partnerships. You can allow YouTube to show advertising at the beginning of your music videos and make money in the process.

In fact, YouTube recently launched a partner program specifically for indie bands. Bands who are accepted will get to add tour dates and "buy" links for music and merchandise and exert further control over the design of their pages. On top of this, their music will be much easier for new fans to find thanks to their new partnership with the ones controlling the search. See how that works? Start thinking like a business and outsource! Advertise! You can apply for consideration at the following link: http://www.youtube.com/musicianswanted

Bloglines - RSS feed aggregator

Netvibes - personalized homepage

Last.FM - customized music consumption (Build a presence here. Create play lists so people can spread the word about your band. This is a viral music website.) Last.fm lies is a music community that builds itself around personalized 'radio stations'. With more than 21 million users, it's a huge community that exists only for people to catch on to new music.

Independent Music Promotions

One feature that is worthwhile is that you can be paid royalties for every song played on the service. There is also the 'Audioscrobbler' which tracks all the music you listen to and builds a profile of your listening habits on your public Last.fm page. You can build a community around your Last.fm profile and help your music spread quickly.

Odeo - create and share audio & podcasts

Streampad - Internet audio player

MP3Tunes - backup and archive your music online

Clipmarks - collaborative web clippings

Dropcash - make your own fundraiser

Twitter - micro blogging what you're up to right now (This site is gaining steam and carries a particular importance these days. Set up a profile here and keep it updated). To keep things simple, Facebook now offers a feature that automatically updates your Twitter every time you update your band's Facebook status. This can be very helpful if you don't like to frequent both sites all the time.

However, it is suggested by many Twitter experts that you always post original statuses in order to keep your followers engaged. Tag relevant companies and people as much as possible with relevant messages. This allows you to reach out to their followers and build your Twitter community that much faster.

Feedburner - customize and enhance your feed

YouSendIt - send big files without clogging email (Ideal for sending digital copies of your album to potential reviewers. Get familiar.) If you end up choosing Bandzoogle as your website host, they also have a feature which allows you to send digital albums free of charge.

Amie Street - price-per-popularity music community

Wordpress - blogging platform

Vimeo - video sharing and management

Imeem - social networking site, like YouTube, though you can stream music and photos as well. Merge your music, videos and photos in order to gain new fans. Your playlists can be rated by others and ranked, which is a definite plus. The top rating playlists on Imeem receive over 2 million plays.

Jumpcut - online video editing and remixing

Reddit - popular links shared and commented

PBWiki - make your own wiki

Feed43 - make an RSS feed out of any site

Dropload - send big files

Diigo - social bookmarking and annotation

Vox - social networking through blogging

Mog - music sharing through blogging

Artistdata - Artist Data could turn out to be a highly valuable timesaver for you. Upload your details to Artist Data and have them sent all over the place – for example, to MySpace, Last.fm, etc. Keep your news distributed and your fans up to date.

Tubemogul - Instead of uploading your video to YouTube and every other video hosting site individually, Tubemogul allows you to upload your video once and they will deliver it to all the relevant video sites for you. You can track your results from there. The basic service is free but for more tracking it will require membership fees.

More Strategies

Blog comments: Comment on other people's blogs. Make sure you include your band's web address so people can check you out. Keep in mind your comments must be relevant to the blog and not for spamming purposes. If your comments are interesting, people are more likely to visit your website.

Email signatures: Make sure every email you send has a signature with your website on it. This is another way to build your profile. For example:

James Marsdon

The Dead Animals – Goth Rock Band from California

www.thedeadanimalsrock.com

jamesmarsdon@thedeadanimalsrock.com

(Insert phone number here)

Posting in forums: Careful with this one! Don't bother setting up fake profiles and answering your own posts about your music. The administrators, and in most cases everyone else, will be able to tell you are doing this and it could ruin your reputation. To participate in forums, follow the blog commenting procedure. Make your posts relevant. Get into conversations about topics you care about. Get people to respect your opinion. And of course, include your website as your signature in every post. People will check you out.

Outsource everything: Why not get as many people promoting you as possible? Use micro-job websites such as **Fiverr.com** to hire people to do everything from write a review to dancing around on a YouTube video while carrying a sign with your band name!

Unique content as a sales pitch: Pitch yourself as a perfect interview subject to as many blogs as possible. Use the term "unique content" in your request. Blogs go crazy over this because it translates to relevant content for their blog with very little effort required on their part. Not many bands promote themselves in this way and it just may help you get on some bigger blogs outside of your main niche.

Podcasts

Podcasting today is pretty much what radio used to be: shows about various topics that anyone can put together, upload as an MP3, and broadcast to the public through RSS. There are all types of podcasts and they differ wildly in size of audience - some with only a few listeners, others with tens of thousands. With podcasting, music and video content is available by subscription download. Once downloaded, it can be viewed or heard at the user's convenience. Users typically use software such as iTunes to subscribe and download the content.

Once downloaded, the files are ready to be listened to.

Getting your music on any podcast is one of the easiest ways to expose your music to potential new fans. In fact, getting played on podcasts could be lucrative to the success or failure of your online promotion campaign. Want to make this actionable and get started right away? Here's how.

Register your music with a Podsafe Collective

Podcasters have set up podsafe music collectives to ensure the music they play is podsafe. This saves them from lawsuits and legal hassles from both artists and record labels. To get on the list, these podsafe music collectives ask musicians to sign up and upload songs that are safe for podcasters to play. By registering and uploading songs, you agree to make your music podsafe under a podsafe license. Some of these collectives include the Podsafe Music Network and Podsafe Audio. Podsafe Audio uses a Creative Commons license. One thing that differentiates many podcasters with the average radio DJ is that podcasters are often eager to hear your music. They do not get paid for what they do and they do it out of a love for music. They tend to appreciate it when artists send their music. Remember, they are independent too, so be personal and get them on your side. Being on the playlist for relevant podcasts can be extremely helpful to getting your band known.

Choose podcasts that are relevant to your style

If you are a groove rock band, don't bother the jazz podcast asking them to check out your music. But do contact any and all podcasts who play your genre. Use the same tactics we talked about in our Behind-the-scenes marketing chapter.

Independent Music Promotions

Promote them in return

Podcasts love cross-promotion. They want more listeners, just like you do. It's a match made in heaven, so no need for all the promotional language. Talk to them like human beings and offer to help however you can in return for them playing your music.

Why not create your own podcast while you're at it? Go viral by yourself!

Another option for you independent musicians is to create your own podcast. It doesn't have to be a simple playlist of your music. You can include a band interview, describe the meaning being your song, show your sense of humour, lash out with your best political rant or announce a contest.

It's easy to do. Here's what you will need:

- A computer

- An MP3 file to podcast

- Music editing/recording software

- Text-editing software

- An RSS text file

- Somewhere online to post your files

Let's assume you already have an original song saved as an MP3 file on your computer. You'll then want to add a voice-over track to complete the show. With free audio software like Audacity, you can quickly record and edit voice-over elements right on your computer. If you have any kind of home studio, you can easily create a higher quality recording.

Once compiled and edited, save the new file as an MP3. To make your file ready to podcast, there is specific ID and naming protocol you must follow.

Yahoo has a very helpful tutorial at http://podcasts.yahoo.com/publish/1, and there's another well-done explanation at

http://www.podcastingnews.com/articles/How-to-Podcast.html.

You will then need to FTP your file to your own website, or use a hosting service like Yahoo! Geocities.

One major benefit of podcasting regularly is that subscribers will automatically get updates whenever you post new episodes. To do this, you have to create an RSS feed for your podcast. The RSS feed alerts subscribers about your updated podcast and allows them to be downloaded immediately.

Music Mp3 Blogs

While some artists set their minds on that feature article in Rolling Stone, the smart ones are emailing all the Music mp3 bloggers (within their relevant style) they can find. Music bloggers are freelance music reviewers who write and share the music they love online. They are usually quite independent though they can tend to have a lot of listeners/subscribers.

Many MP3 blogs do allow submissions, so submitting your music to get reviewed not only is great exposure for your music, but a good review will help you get blurbs for your press kit. Let your promotion feed itself. The more you get talked about, the more you have to post on your site networks and blogs (your social networking). More people find you and the positive cycle continues.

Remember that the bloggers are the mouths that speak to today's music listener. If they talk about you in a positive light, you are on your way. We advise that you visit Hype Machine immediately and start searching the thousands of mp3 blogs to find where you fit in.

Film and TV placement

Getting your music into a film or television show is great publicity. You can try to search for these opportunities independently or alternatively, you can sign up for one of many website services that connects independent musicians with independent filmmakers. Here are a few to check out and decide for yourself. Most of them have minimal membership fees. Try it out and see what works for you.

www.versusmedia.com - Provides opportunities for film music placement, music licensing, publicity and promotion services.

www.beatpick.com - A website that licenses music for film and television use. They have a different profit breakdown than some of their competitors. Artists get 50% of the profit.

www.filmmusic.net - Similar website to the others with extensive job listings and an $11.95 monthly fee.

shootingpeople.org – A large community of filmmakers frequent this website. It can provide a place where you can get in touch with filmmakers potentially in need of your music.

Guerrilla Marketing

Contacting Bigger Media and playing by the rules better than anyone else

How will the big guns notice you? Contacting larger media outlets can be trickier, and there are some cases where you will definitely want to follow the strict submission procedures. We're not backing off our "Behind-the-scenes marketing strategy" by any means! We're just saying people who write for Rolling Stone tend to be less accessible. So if you are by chance submitting a news tip or asking for coverage by emailing editors@rollingstone.com (their actual news tip email), then you'll want to follow a few guidelines.

For the message title, all capitals is a no-no. "Next big thing" is also a no-no. It's common sense really. Think of what you would typically delete in your own inbox and don't send those types of titles!

A perfectly suitable title would go something like "New Stoner Rock Band from California". This way they know exactly what the message is about and it's not belligerent.

In the body of the message, address them by name whenever you can.

Be polite. They will appreciate it.

Introduce your act and get right to the point.

Check your grammar.

Your first email to a bigger media outlet should be more of a request than a full-blown release.

Keep it short. If they want more information they will ask for it.

Include links and contact information for them to investigate.

Don't email mp3's straight away. Wait until they request it back from you. Even better than this is to include a secure link that contains all your media. Set yourself up with Dropbox or Mediafire, and put everything in clean zip files. Blogs should be able to get your new album, press photos, bio and music video within one or two clicks.

Follow up ONCE. Do this anywhere from 5 business days to 2 weeks after sending the initial email.

Become an easy target.

You need to be easily reachable. This does not just mean your Contact section on your website. Make sure you include your contact information on everything you send out, including your emails, newsletters and press releases. You don't want to miss the call because your phone number wasn't provided.

NICHE YOURSELF

Don't you hate it when you ask someone what kind of music they listen to and they reply "Everything?" This usually means they are not passionate about ANY music, but are happy with whatever comes along on the radio. Are these people interesting? Would you want to get into a deep discussion about the meaning behind Pink Floyd's "The Wall" with one of these people? No!

DON'T BE THAT BAND.

Describe yourself!

Carve your niche and carve it well!

Say what you sound like! Use your influences if you like. Be proud of it.

Old School off-line promotion

1. Have a hook.

Just like your favorite Smashing Pumpkins track has a killer chorus hook, your band's story needs to have a hook.

A hook must get people's attention right away. One sentence instead of twenty.

"Los Angeles rock band eats live goat on stage"

"Anarchism is alive and well and it lives in Seattle"

"London rockers express hate for Nickelback, release new CD"

Those are extreme examples but we can guarantee you would at least

Check out the live goat one!

2. Don't give up.

You are the salesperson, the marketer for your band, so you must know what you're selling inside and out, and you must also know your customers (radio, media, etc). Respect what they need from you and follow through on it.

Be persistent. Call back. Follow up. And do it all in a personable way that gets them on your side.

3. Be honest.

People aren't stupid. It will help you in the long run if you are honest and upfront with everyone. Back up your claims.

Performing Rights Organizations

Performing rights organizations like BMI and ASCAP in America and SOCAN in Canada make it their job to collect on money owed to musicians from all revenue sources (TV, film, radio, live performances, and internet airplay such as podcasts).

When someone uses a song or piece you wrote, you are supposed to get paid. If it's a great opportunity, occasionally you can sign up for cross-promotion purposes, but make sure you get something out of it! Performing rights organizations gather up these monies, take a fee for doing so, and send you checks. If you make enough connections, you can eventually base a good portion of your income on this.

You have to register with one of the organizations to get this money. It's free to register and you can do it online, but you can only join one, not all. The two major organizations in the United States are:

BMI: www.bmi.com

ASCAP: www.ascap.com

Check them out and decide for yourself which one to sign up for.

Cue Sheets

In order to get paid for having your music used in a film, the filmmaker has to turn in "cue sheets" to ASCAP and BMI. Cue sheets list the name of the movie, the name of the songs used, how many seconds of the song were used, at what point they are used in the film, the composer, and the composer's affiliation (ASCAP or BMI) and the name of their publishing company. (If you don't have a publishing company, you can make up your own company name when you join, and that is your publishing company. If you are your own publisher, you should join both as a composer and a publisher, and list both when you turn in info for cue sheets.

On a major company's production, they will definitely turn in cue sheets. On an independent film, you may have to get in touch with the producer or director and make sure he turns one in. You can even turn them in yourself.

For ASCAP's tutorial on Cue Sheets go to:

http://www.ascap.com/playback/2005/winter/cuesheets.html

For BMI's guide go to www.bmi.com

http://www.bmi.com/library/brochures/cuesheet.asp

Branding

Many bands and musicians try to hide themselves behind an air of mystique when representing themselves or promoting online. Artistically, a lot of artists try to follow the example of cryptic bands like Tool or Radiohead when promoting. This can work if you come up with the perfect marketing campaign, but normally it isolates you or produces the opposite effect of what you're looking for. Instead of appearing mysterious and larger-than-life, people view you as pretentious and difficult to relate to. The reason some bigger bands can get away with it is anticipation created by millions of dollars worth of promotion and years of building their brand. Some bands waste time on forums under fake aliases, hiding their identities in fear that it would ruin everything if they revealed themselves. This creates a lack of trust and it never really helps much.

So how can you, as an independent musician, create trust and build YOUR brand?

Reveal Your Identity

The bands that stand out these days are the ones that show themselves to their fan bases. This means you have an online presence under your own name. It means you are accessible for your fans to talk to. It means you build an online presence for yourself. It means you are honest and open. Be confident. Stand behind your message. What do you have to hide?

Work from the gutter, on the frontlines, money or no money.

Use often-overlooked techniques to give your music wider exposure.

Build a following one fan at a time.

Celebrate each small success and USE IT. Use each success to gain you another one, to move forward.

Exploit your story. Get it out there. Be extreme and different.

Give stuff away. Don't expect anything if you're stingy.

Create Podcast & Radio ID's and Intros

This is something that most bands don't do, and it costs them a lot of airplay. Independent radio shows and podcasts are always looking for bands to record custom song intro's and radio ID's to promote their show. An example of this is "Hi, this is James from Vancouver rock band The Slimy Snails and you're listening to the Non Stop Rock Podcast!"

When you initially contact the show, why not offer to record an ID for them? They will be 50 percent more likely to play your band, and much more keen on supporting you in the future.

Putting in this effort shows them that:

1) You took the time to listen to their show. You show that you're a real person.
2) B) You are taking the time to help the podcaster or radio host promote themselves. It shows them you're not just in it to get yourself out there. You want to return the favor.

GIVE AWAY FREE STUFF

This deserves its own section, as it's important for the spreading of your product. Websites (in relevant genres), music blogs, magazines, podcasts and internet radio appreciate nothing more than receiving product. This can be in the form of CD's, T-shirts, stickers, or any other products you want to throw in the package.

Yes, this will cost you some shipping fees, but it is critical that you invest in it. Each website that advertises your "Contest giveaway", first of all, becomes a dependable ally for you. Sending them product makes them much more likely to post features on your band, as well as the latest news.

The posting of the contest alone spreads the word about your band. The public perception of contests like these is normally associated with bigger bands, so it looks very good!

And of course the winners of these contests and everyone who checks out your website in the meantime, become new fans from all over the world.

So, don't sweat the cash. Once your album shipment is in, make sure you send multiple copies to all the hundreds of valuable allies you've gained through using the steps contained in our guide. Being generous and treating your "family" well pays off in spades.

RESEARCH YOUR GENRE (AND SUB-GENRES)

This topic isn't discussed too extensively in other books. Unless you are one of those delusional bands who think they are a "space rock/jazz/funk/death metal/fusion/pop/contemporary hybrid", you most likely have a few genres you could be listed under. The reason we mention sub-genres is because they are absolutely valid. Many rock bands, for example, may have tracks that could be played in rock, indie rock, alternative rock, metal, industrial, progressive and hardcore formats.

This may be a stretch for bands that have the same sound all the way through their respective albums, but you get the idea. The more genres you embrace, the wider your potential audience.

It's also important to research your potential media audience, because it's a big world out there and it's not all about Billboard Magazine.

There are specialty independent publications for everything from noise rock to eclectic progressive fantasy metal. They are putting their time into it for the love of the music, so get in touch with them. If you personalize it, you have a good shot. This is the way to build up your press section. It's all real people.

Another bonus: Guess who reads these strange music blogs and independent publications who cater to niche audiences? Well, you guessed it. Niche audiences. People who are fanatical about their music and trust the sources they get their information from. Get IN with these people. Befriend them and treat them well.

Resources

You may want to search the relevant online directories or pick up the latest Indie Band Bible, but here are some sites you will definitely want to get in touch with.

Hypebot – www.hypebot.com

Hypebot is one of the most informative music business websites currently on the net. Keep a close eye on this site for industry news, music marketing advice, and opinions from various knowledgeable sources.

Music Think Tank – www.musicthinktank.com

Owned and edited by the same person as Hypebot, Music Think Tank offers endless insight into music promotion, with fresh content from both regular and guest posters.

Berklee School of Music - www.berkleemusic.com

Berklee is a very respected music school with courses covering everything from song writing to the music business.

DIY Musician from CDBaby - http://diymusician.cdbaby.com/

Relevant and simple advice from CDBaby's blog.

Independent Music Promotions

Make It In Music – www.makeitinmusic.com

Another informative industry advice website.

The Indie Bible – www.indiebible.com

The Indie Bible provides an excellent resource for independent artists looking for reviews, airplay, distribution, press or advice. To go beyond the music blogs checklist that Hype Machine will offer, pick up a copy.

The Indie Venue Bible – www.indiebible.com

The Indie Venue Bible is a comprehensive venue database created to assist independent musicians with the tough job of booking tours. If you are planning a tour on your own, this is another MUST HAVE. Released by the Indie Bible team, this book is specifically for touring artists and contains more venues than you could possibly ever play. Even better, the venues are expecting you to get in touch.

Artists in Music Awards – www.aimusicawards.com

Founded Mikey Jayy has a deep passion for independent music of all genres, and he dedicates his days and nights to promoting it through his popular radio show and his Los Angeles-based Artists in Music Awards, which is open to artists of all genres worldwide.

Music XRay – www.musicxray.com

Music XRay is a A & R and opportunities website for independent musicians. Artists can submit their music for major record label consideration, licensing (film, video game, tv) opportunities, consultations, reviews, airplay, promotional campaigns and press coverage just to name a few.

WHOA Magazine – www.whoamagazine.co

Ever since I first started working with WHOA Magazine, the drive and enthusiasm of CEO Anthony "Train" Caruso has blown me away. They are one of the few publications at their level who are genuinely open to independent artists. In fact, they fill their pages with them as well as interview them every weekday on their WHOA 100 Radio show. With the new WHOA Label launched, there's no stopping this company.

Jamsphere Magazine – www.jamsphere.com

Jamsphere is a multi-faceted company who I have had nothing but wonderful experiences with. Dedicated to the success of independent artists to the point that their services are constantly expanding their reach, you can be guaranteed that all quality artists are given a fair chance here. They syndicate their reviews to ensure added exposure. Coupled with their radio show and corresponding website, their brand new magazine and low advertising rates, Jamsphere.com is a highly recommended hub for any serious independent artist.

I Am Entertainment Magazine - www.iaemagazine.com

They're ambitious and they run a very professional publication. They also provide independent artists with one of the best opportunities for both reviews and advertising, with among the lowest and most reasonable rates I've seen. Taking care of the other side of the business, they properly promote their magazine, recently going into print in a time when most are shying away.

Middle Tennessee Music – www.midtnmusic.com

Middle Tennessee Music is chalk full of valuable advice for musicians. They also provide high quality artist reviews and interviews as well.

Vandala Concepts Magazine – www.vandalaconcepts.com

This publication is open to independent artists, and cover as many as any other I've seen. On top of this, they provide just about every service imaginable to serious artists.

SKOPE Magazine – www.skopemag.com

SKOPE Magazine is another publication dedicated solely to independent music. They actually give independent artists a chance, so this is a great place to start for any artist looking for exposure or advertising.

Penseyeview – www.penseyeview.com

One of our favourite publications and an excellent supporter of independent music through their daily music features.

Target Audience Magazine - www.targetaudiencemagazine.com

Covering a mixture of major and independent artists, I've had nothing but positive experiences with Target Audience Magazine. I encourage you to read and support the publication.

This Is Vibes – www.thisisvibes.com

An independent music site spanning all genres with a special focus on hip hop and r&b.

Music Emissions – www.musicemissions.com

Music Emissions is a massive independent music community reviewing both indie and major artists. They offer paid reviews and the service is very professional.

Independent Music Promotions

Indie Band Guru – www.indiebandguru.com

Exactly as the title suggests, site creator Keith Pro is the real deal, always striving to help indie acts.

The Real Musician – www.therealmusician.com

Offering everything from music marketing advice to an in-depth guide to producing music with Reason, Andrew Muller's The Real Musician website has grown into a high traffic institution for a reason. It's helpful.

All Songs Considered - http://www.npr.org/programs/asc/submissions/

All Songs Considered is a high influential program put on by NPR, and they give all artists a chance. Be sure to follow the instructions to a tee, and make sure your product is ready.

Kings of A&R – www.kingsofar.com

Kings of A&R is very popular publication. Artists featured here often move on to big things.

Musicperk – www.musicperk.com

Many artists make the mistake of sticking to their home town when looking for press. Few think to look towards India, where one of the coolest and most helpful websites, Musicperk, can be found.

Totally Fuzzy – www.totallyfuzzy.blogspot.com

Totally Fuzzy is the name. Music discovery is the game. Have an album stream ready? How about a new music video? This is the website for you.

Hellhound Music – www.hellhoundmusic.com

Hellhound Music is a top notch rock (and surrounding genres) website without any snobbery whatsoever. They're a friendly and enthusiastic group of folks who in my experience have an extremely positive attitude towards independent acts.

Ultima Music Blog – www.ultimamusicblog.net

Covering rock, electronic, industrial, metal, punk, progressive and surrounding genres, Ultima is a wonderful publication.

Independent Music Promotions

Feedback Fury – www.feedbackfury.com

Fast and furious, this rock, punk, alternative and metal website gained attention by conducting unique interviews with up-and-coming artists, as well as stars like Henry Rollins.

Speakercone – www.speakercone.net

Offering a wide range of services for independent artists, Speakercone is run by Michael Finney, a musician and entrepreneur who loves passionate artists.

Ampkicker – www.ampkicker.com

They've been supporting indie bands since their inception and show no signs of slowing down.

Music Review Unsigned – www.musicreviewunsigned.com

One of the best independent music publications online.

Blog Critics – www.blogcritics.com

They cater to all genres. Seek out a reviewer and contact him with a pitch.

Spoutfire – www.spoutfire.com

Send in your submissions for their 'Music Interlude' section.

Vents Magazine – www.ventsmagazine.com

Covering all genres and very much open to independent acts.

Bandbucket.com – www.bandbucket.com

Opportunities abound on this alternative music site.

The Noise Beneath the Apple - www.thenoisebeneaththeapple.com

Wonderful independent music website covering artists in New York and internationally, with an added focus on the art of busking.

Nanobot Rock – www.nanobotrock.com

High quality and very approachable music review site supporting quality independent artists.

Music Connection Magazine – www.musicconnection.com

Join their AMP network to get reviewed.

Technorati Music Blogs Database - http://technorati.com/blogs/directory/entertainment/music/

Technorati is the largest blog tracker in the world. Their music blog database has 8,000 music blogs. It's VERY possible that some of them would be interested in your band.

No Depression – www.nodepression.com

No Depression is a hub for the country and Americana music communities. This very popular publication has turned itself into a social network where independent musicians are encouraged to sign up and post their music and news releases. Don't hesitate to contact the industry professionals and reviewers who frequent the site.

Garageband – www.garageband.com

The world's largest independent music community. This site offers the potential to get reviewed by new fans and fellow musicians.

Drowned in Sound – www.drownedinsound.com

Appeal to the individual reviewers here. This site is lucrative and influential.

Blabbermouth – www.blabbermouth.net

Blabbermouth is a great place to break a press release for rock/metal bands. Get it posted here and it will mysteriously show up in a lot of other places.

Band Weblogs – www.bandweblogs.com

Band weblogs will post your press releases provided they are relevant and well-written. Make sure you return the generosity by making your releases newsworthy and informative.

Artist Direct – www.artistdirect.com

Get as involved as you can with this website. They offer a variety of features.

Antimusic – www.antimusic.com

We've found Antimusic to be an excellent rock music news website, and they accept news releases from bands. Even better, they offer features on independent artists.

Independent Music Promotions

Pure Grain Audio – www.puregrainaudio.com

This website supports indie artists, but unlike other "indie" sites, it has a wide audience, and garners press with many major artists as well. It's an excellent site to get involved with.

Chart Attack - www.chartattack.com

Contrary to the site's title, you don't need to be on the charts to be covered. Indie bands can be found all over this site.

MI2N - www.mi2n.com/

Ah yes! Post your press releases here and never look back!

Alternative Press – www.altpress.com

Another popular publication that covers indie bands in it's online format.

The Daily Swarm - www.thedailyswarm.com

Music news and headlines.

NPR – www.npr.org

Even though it's the top music site as ranked by Google, they do have a section called "All Songs Considered", which accepts independent music submissions.

Ultimate Guitar - www.ultimate-guitar.com/news

You do play guitar, right? Well, send them some news! Approach them with a relevant article idea.

Play Louder - www.playlouder.com

Music reviews and news website.

Taxi – www.taxi.com

"Get your music to the right people" is their slogan. Taxi works to get your music submitted for film, television or advertising placement. Give it a try and see if it works for you.

Large Hearted Boy - http://blog.largeheartedboy.com

If this boy digs you, you've got an audience.

Music for Robots - http://music.for-robots.com/

Music for Robots is an extremely popular indie music blog. This website provides a very helpful list of music blogs for you to promote to.

Bonus Article:

"Can we get in Pitchfork?"

At Independent Music Promotions we are lucky enough to be exposed to an extremely wide variety of independent bands, and it often seems the difference between a band rising fast, sinking like a stone or staying motionless in place comes down to the ideas and beliefs held by the band members themselves. Just like in life, ideas, philosophies and belief systems can cause us a lot of trouble internally and externally, leading us to do and think all kinds of irrational things. Some of the following list will be concrete things that many artists tend not to think about, and some of it will include harmful ideas they hold dear.

All of them I see firsthand, and often enough to be inspired to share this article.

1) "All or Nothing"

Possibly due to growing up with long-held cultural expectations going all the way back to Elvis Presley and the Beatles, our collective idea of what it is to "be in a band" or "to make it" generally involves visions of superstars gracing the stage in front of 50,000 or so obsessed followers. It's fine and good to have an image in your mind of your goal. The problem is, this goal, if held too close and without the proper neutrality, can taint all the building blocks along the way and cause bands to implode early when they were just on the verge of getting somewhere. Artists who start off wanting everything nearly always grossly underestimate the work involved, and this leads to disillusionment and despair. There's no such thing in reality as "all or nothing". You are where you are so start from there.

2) "I'm a True Artist"

This is a true poison. If you're an honest, true artist, I congratulate you. In my view, you're a wonderful thing for this world. However, just BE an honest artist. Don't THINK you are one. It will get in your way, trust me. It's the same as the man on the path to enlightenment who thinks "I'm a great yogi". He won't achieve his goal. Thinking "I'm a true artist" tends to solidify subconscious beliefs about lack of success, "the Man", and the army of commercial sods out there that you're up against. It can make you feel alone in a music industry that sometimes seems to be a more dangerous environment than the Democratic Republic of the Congo. Don't let yourself get polarized. The Doors are considered by many to be true artists, and yet they also had the business drive to make it. They called in to Los Angeles radio requesting "Break on Through" to get their foot in the door. They didn't expect anyone to find them because of their unique gifts.

3) "We have no money"

That may be true, and everyone has their stories as to why they're in that situation. People have stories about why they're in ANY given situation; why they're lazy, why they're sick, why they're angry, why they don't trust people, why they are religious, why they are stressed, why they believe humanity is doomed…and many of our stories are quite rational and justified. We re-enforce them by repeating them over and over to anyone willing to listen.

But it doesn't help.

The tough thing to accept, and this really is a bitter pill to swallow, is this. No one cares about your story. They may understand. They may empathize. But no one really cares. Once you know that, once you TRULY know that, it's liberating. You can face who you actually are and where you actually are with courage instead of excuses.

Your band is a BUSINESS. In no other business are people allowed to say "I don't have money but I want success". The landlord would kick you out in a second. It's only independent bands who have such an issue with investing in themselves.

4) "Can we get in Pitchfork?"

I've been asked this question by many artists who are just starting out, and of course, there is always that chance. However, there seems to be a looming expectation attached to the question that has some troubling residue. One artist advised me that he would accept interview requests from publications like Pitchfork or Rolling Stone, but I would have to get his permission for "smaller publications". Do you see the issue here? If you don't embrace and respect ALL the media, including the tiniest independent music blogs, you'll most likely be very disappointed with your results. Most bands contact the top 50 music blogs after finding a list somewhere and ignore the rest of the blogosphere. In their minds, they're simply too good to waste their time on small publications.

5) "We're very coachable. Mold us!"

Not everyone will agree with me on this point, and it's fine because my point of view is subjective, and based on the kinds of music I personally value. I often receive submissions from bands who quite obviously try to sound like their idols, whether that be Creed, Jack White, Lil Wayne, or Nickelback (shudder). While this can end up being a successful strategy for some, most media personnel will just see you as a clone. If you really get to know publications like Popmatters, Consequence of Sound, Pitchfork, and Filter Magazine, or checking the latest festival lineups, you'll see a trend happening that leans heavily towards the innovative.

This goes against what most music promotion guides tell us. They tell you to be coachable and to listen to industry guidance. Write radio friendly songs. But I don't think that's true. You need to be genuine, and it's not genuine to copy someone or try to cater to an industry for financial or vanity reasons.

Don't compromise your art. Run with it. Do something vital, dangerous, meaningful, and most of all, honest.

6) "Wait in line and you'll get your share"

With the prevalence of endless music authorities of every kind, independent artists have in some cases adopted a "wait in line" mentality that can be quite harmful. You've submitted your music to every blog on Hype Machine and applied for every opportunity on Sonicbids. No one has responded. Now what?

Most music publications receive hundreds of submissions per day. More than likely they won't even listen to your music. Some blogs appear to be open to independent artists but are effectively shut down to the outside world. The idea of sending your album to all the respective "review queues" and waiting for something to happen, playing by the rules as it may be, just doesn't work.

There is a commonly held subconscious belief amongst musicians that pictures a level playing field of sorts. The music industry, as we like to think of it, is a giant, endless panel populated by A&R representatives ready to listen to every band, one at a time. But the reality is that very few people have the time or will make the time to listen to your music, let alone spread it in any way. You need to understand this and take control of your own progress.

Reach out personally to any genre expert who could possibly help you. Take the time to personally connect with as many people as possible. Hire freelancers to get on your side and possibly cover your band's new release. Offer something in return. Donate to blogs you respect and they will appreciate it. If you support them, they are much more likely to support you. Yes, I said it. It's the truth. Most bands think each website has a whole bunch of writers waiting with all the time in the world to write blogs about them, but people generally want something for their time, whether it's money to keep doing what they're doing, cross-promotion, acknowledgement of their work, or just an actual human conversation instead of a robotic press release.

Advertise. Research micro-job websites. Reach out to respected licensing companies. Contact writer's individually and let them know which pieces of their's you enjoyed rather than going through the main channels. Start a blog of your own and offer cross-promotion. Follow up when appropriate. Target non-music specific publications that have music sections.

There are thousands of things you could be doing while you're waiting in line, but never just wait.

Bonus Article
Independent Artists Working Brilliantly Towards Success

by Samuel Marcus & Jennifer Thorington
www.workingbrilliantly.com

Indie artists in today's world have a huge advantage. Music promotion and sales are now in their court and the control of their careers are in their hands. This is a blessing to most, since the creative control and success of their music is reliant on their personal overall focus, determination and belief in themselves versus a huge record label controlling all aspects of their lives. But, on the other hand, it poses a problem for those artists who have a harder time organizing themselves or running the business side of their career. Thankfully, there are many options available to help with this, such as managers, PR companies and sites like Reverbnation and Constant Contact that help organize their fans, assist with press outreach, promote new releases, videos, etc. and keep all their information in one easy place. Websites are even easier to build and financial support can be raised through sites like Wix and Kickstarter.

Financial success is a huge factor in an artist's ability to pursue their art full time. It is more than possible in this day and age for an independent artist to not only recoup their investment, but also support a lifestyle that is in alignment with what they dream for themselves. It takes time, focus, perseverance, work, creativity and unwavering confidence in their ability to succeed.

We have noticed over the years that a stumbling block for musicians is giving up or letting go of a project too soon. Now this is not a bid to get independent musicians deeper into financial debt with their project, but a simple philosophy on perseverance:

A release has a long shelf life. A client will too often give up on their project because a) they have had little return from the press world b) they have had a discouraging response from press or c) they are overly excited about their new project and are therefore dismissive of their previous one.

The truth is that press is a cumulative process in which you or your manager or publicist works their ass off to get peoples' attention. Unless you are working with payola outlets or have some insanely juicy publicity angle, good music takes a while to get heard, processed and put into print. More often than not, you have to water the proverbial flower and over time it will, indeed, bloom into something impressionable. That is unless you stomp on the sprout before it fully forms.

Another good analogy is that of drops of water in a pond. The ramifications of releasing an album occur over time, echoing out into the world through exposure and word of mouth. The more drops of water, the bigger the impact, the more chances to reach the shore.

Artists should be supporting their release in as many creative ways as possible. One idea could be to create a music video to support every song on the album and each video should be publicized in a compelling way, bringing people back to the album via interest in the video. Another could be simply visiting different hangouts on the Internet; starting clever conversations with potential fans and channeling them back to an amazingly well put together web site.

The biggest success we have seen is with bands that put out their material and don't look back. That is to say, they never question if they did the right thing, letting the chips fall where they may. That doesn't mean they neglect their release, it means they move forward into more endeavors that support it like touring, viral media, positive thinking and continual fan and press outreach.

Bonus Interview with Stuart Epps

It was a true honour for me to have the chance to speak with the legendary record producer/engineer Stuart Epps (www.stuartepps.co.uk), who has worked with artists such as Led Zeppelin, Elton John, George Harrison, Bill Wyman, Oasis, Twisted Sister, Robbie Williams, Jeff Beck, Paul Rodgers and many others. Starting his music career at the age of 15 in 1967, Stuart has over 40 years of first-hand experience in the ever-changing music industry.

Aspiring artists and producers alike should find this interview both sobering and inspiring. We talked about some of the main issues confronting the industry today and his answers were fascinating. The main message I personally took from it is that we all have sometimes rigid perceptions of what the "music industry" should be and what it owes us for our efforts, but, as George Gershwin would say, "It ain't necessarily so." Success in any facet of the business is difficult, but it is definitely possible. In some ways, not much has changed, and that should be a relief to many. Without further delay, Stuart Epps!

Mr. Epps, it's an honor to speak with you and thank you for your contributions to music. Please share with our readers what you've been up to lately. I understand that you accept independent artist submissions for production, mixing and mastering, which is a stellar opportunity.

Hi James. It's incredible, really. I've been in this business for 40 years now and I thought I'd seen everything, done everything and been everywhere, but it's the amazing thing about this business I'm in that I'm often finding myself in situations I haven't been in before; whether it's a different band, different music or different sounds, and obviously the music business is changing and has changed dramatically.

At the moment, via a great music website called Music XRay I have been mixing bands and artist's home recordings, which is something I never imagined I'd be doing. To be honest I got a bit fed up with lack of budgets and trying to get artists to record in commercial studios. Anyway, with the invention of the internet I'm in touch with bands and the internet has brought us together – musicians and artists and producers from all over the world.

So it's pooling resources, and what I'm finding myself doing now is taking the waves from artist's home recordings and mixing them, as well as sometimes adding my own production ideas such as adding other instruments and enhancing what they've already achieved, which is working out great. I'm enjoying doing it. Sometimes artists aren't the easiest to deal with face to face. This way I'm not always having to. Sometimes I don't even speak to anyone. We're just communicating via their music, which isn't a bad thing really. That's working out well and I've been very busy with that. I'm still working with artists in my own studio and in commercial studios but as I said, unfortunately budgets are on the decrease so remixing is a good way to "carry on the good work".

Independent Music Promotions

What is the best way for someone interested in music production to learn how to do what you do?

Interesting question because music is so huge now, really – bigger than ever before and everyone is making music it would seem. It's promoted on the TV with all your X Factor style shows where everyone is singing away and playing furiously, and live music is bigger than ever before. So everyone wants to learn how to be a music producer it would seem, and I've been lecturing to music schools via Skype in Canada and across the world about this. There are many thousands of colleges that are teaching engineering and music production and of course I'm all for it.

In my day, the only way to learn was really hands on starting at the bottom in a recording studio or a publisher. In my case it was a demo studio and you'd learn engineering and somehow work your way up. Obviously there is a lot more available now as you can actually go to schools to learn that. Hands on is the best way as well. With home recording facilities you can experiment at home, with your friends and with bands. I'm always talking about what separates an engineer from someone who wants to do music production. It's a fascinating subject which is too lengthy to go into here, but they are very different things to learn how to do. For music production, the best thing to do would be to go to a college and jump into it as soon as possible with friends, with bands, with home recording, and learn as much as you can.

Please share your thoughts on the controversial issue of free file sharing and its effects on independent artists.

With the invention of the internet it's incredible that you can record a demo or a track in the morning and by the evening have it finished, then promote it through all the various music sites. Of course I think that it would be nice to make money out of it, but at that early stage I think just getting people to listen is a good thing, really. There's so much music out there that you can't really charge for these things until you become a little bit more well-known and maybe your music has evolved and gotten that much better. Then, maybe you can charge for it, but that's just the same as it was in the 60's and 70's.

A new band starting out was not likely to get paid in a pub or a club. If they made a demo, they probably would have to pay for it. Good luck trying to sell it, too. It's not really any different in that respect. It's just that everyone assumes these days that if you make something one day you should be able to sell it the next day somewhere or other. The main thing is – none of us really thought about the money when we were making music in the 60's or 70's. If you start out at age 15 or 16 or even earlier, you're not thinking in monetary terms. You're just thinking "I want to play music", and if money comes along that's a complete bonus, but this was when the music industry was in its infancy. It wasn't such a huge industry as it is now. I understand that everyone wants to make money from it but I think the fact is that there are so many more people listening to music than ever before. It's become a cheaper item. The whole thing has been cheapened to a certain extent, but because it's in such vast quantities it sort of makes up for it in that respect.

Is the music industry evolving or collapsing? Does it matter?

It's definitely evolving. It's always been evolving. Revolving and evolving…it's probably more revolving now as music just seems to go around in circles with the technology and the different styles of bands. It does seem that there's very little that comes along now that seems to be completely new. It always seems to be somewhat of a rehash of some of the old music. It's just reinvented. People say that the music industry is finished or has collapsed, and certainly the old music industry has collapsed pretty much. The giant record companies are obviously feeling the pressure from the internet, and that's a good thing, really. The only way that you could get a record deal or get your music heard in my day was through a record company or a publisher and very much through the establishment that was set up, which was hard to break into.

Now artists can record a record in their bedroom in the morning and have it beamed out to whoever is there to listen by the evening. That's something that didn't exist when I started, so it's definitely evolving. It's difficult to make money from making records, I suppose. That's what we're talking abut. It's not difficult to make music and it's not difficult to get it heard, really. You can have your own radio station if there's people there to listen. It's possible.

Making money out of the music business and making it a career is not so easy, but then again it never was. Just like any other industry it's very difficult. I would say that it's an extremely exciting time. The live music industry is bigger than ever. There are more bands. There are more artists. There's more people playing live than ever before, and that's an incredible thing. Who would have thought that would have ever been the case in the 60's, or certainly the 80's when it was mainly electronic music. So that's a great thing and I think that the music industry at the moment is more exciting than ever.

Independent Music Promotions

Many artists don't seem to know how to promote themselves properly. What are some of the most common mistakes you see artists make all the time?

It's very difficult. I tend to go for the old, traditional ways which are music publishers and record companies, but then obviously there's MySpace and Facebook. There are literally hundreds of thousands of ways for the individual to promote themselves across the internet with all the various music sites. I think it takes the same tenacity that was needed years ago. The only thing is, life is a bit easier now generally.

People aren't as ruthless now as they used to be in getting their music heard. It was a question of getting out of the house. "How do I get out of the house? How do I leave home? I'm going to go join a band and we'll tour all over the place as long as we don't have to be at home, and as long as we're playing our music". I think that some of that has gone out of individual artists ideas, really. I mean, everyone thinks that you can just make a record in the morning and tomorrow it will be number 1; everyone will be buying it and everyone will be watching you on YouTube and you'll be on X Factor, and everyone tends to want immediate success without putting in as much of the hard work and technical ability or musicality that is required to make great music. It's only when you make great music that you will get a great reaction, and you'll find that you probably don't have to promote yourself.

A lot of the artists that I work with – it took them years, really, to achieve any sort of status. You've got to be dedicated and single-minded. Never give up and never let anything stand in your way. These are the things that are required to help promote your music.

It seems that you have found innovative and collaborative ways to continuously be successful with what you do. Do you have any advice for young producers as well as artists who may be stuck in old models of thinking? (For example, many artists obsess over the decrease of album sales but fail to educate themselves on the benefits of licensing or advertising.)

If we're talking about well-known bands, it is a fact that record sales have decreased. There is a lot of pirating and downloading that still goes on, so obviously even the successful bands aren't selling in the quantities they used to. At the same time, ticket sales are absolutely huge for big bands and that's become the new way for artists to make money. In the early days, the gig was really a promotional tool for the CD and now that's completely reversed. The CD is the promotional tool for the live gig, where then the famous band can go ahead and charge $200 a ticket whereas the CD is only likely to be $20, so it's changed a lot in that respect. I mean, it's always been about promotion. That's where the record companies were vital, really…that whole system of signing a new artist, nurturing them, paying for it as it went along, recording demos, promoting…

I was in there working with Elton John right from the beginning working for Dick James, and a whole team of us…40, 50 people working every day, really, to try and make Elton John a famous artist and to increase record sales, and his whole career, so it's not an easy situation for someone to do on their own. It's almost impossible I would say, but if you're determined enough and you use the tools that are available (which weren't available then), you just have to keep at it and it's possible to get your name out there. You've got to be very dedicated, and beyond all those things, it's about having a great product. You have to have a product that stands out not necessarily quality wise or production wise but depth-wise, the writing and the musicianship. Any great artist who has the right tools will come through in the end. It's just a matter of time.

Is music more difficult to promote these days? Do you feel the market is oversaturated?

It's a very good question. When I started off, music was not something that everyone was into and I suppose you felt that you were part of a select few that made music or recorded music. Maybe there was that magic about it, the idea that "it's only us that know about it", and now everyone seems to be talking about it. If we had a pair of headphones to listen to music with, that was unusual. Now you get on the train and everyone has got a pair of headphones on, but I just think it's great actually. It's just great to see everyone doing what we hoped everyone would do, and that's listening to music and making music.

I don't know about the term 'oversaturated'. There's a lot of still not very good music and there's very few things that ARE great. Maybe that's a good thing as well. To make great music and be a great artist isn't easy. It is difficult. It IS possible but it still takes the same amount of talent that it always took, and you still can't "make a silk purse out of a pig's ear", so to speak. No matter what technology comes along, it's still not possible to be great unless you are truly great. It's just like any other art, really, whether it's painting or sculpting. It doesn't matter how many people have a go at it. There's still only going to be certain people who will succeed at it and are great at it. It doesn't matter how many people make music or get involved in music. It seems that quality wins out in the end…hopefully.

You've worked with some of the greats such as Led Zeppelin and Elton John. In your opinion, is musical greatness something that has to come about naturally, or is tenacity the necessary ingredient?

It's a great question, and I'm lucky to say that having seen it happen, I think I have an answer. Of course, musical talent is important first and foremost. Being a great singer, songwriter, and musician – if you have all those 3 that's very, very rare but that's definitely going to get you somewhere. That's for sure. If you're a great singer, songwriter and a great performer that's when you get the greats. You mentioned Elton John and Led Zeppelin, some of the greats who I've been fortunate enough to work with – they had those 3 talents. But also, extremely important and just as important, if not more important, is determination, having an inner strength and a wanting to succeed in the business of music. To have it happen. To make it big. To question everything, really.

If you do that all the way along the line then chances are you will come out with something special. If you're writing a song and you think "No, it's got to be better. It's got to be better. It can still be better." then you'll write a better song. If you're trying to become a better singer, you hear yourself recorded and you think "No, I can sing better than that. I want to sing better than that. I'm going to sing better than that." Same with guitar playing, piano playing, drums – everything. It's critical as a musician to get better and better.

Independent Music Promotions

Some things I find difficult with young musicians if they want to be great at everything. They want to be a great drummer and a great singer and a great producer and a great engineer. They seem to want to be good at every part of every facet of the music business, which isn't the case with some of those people I've mentioned. In the early days, musicians let managers and producers get on with what they did while they got on with what they did the best they knew how, and I think that's something to learn from, really. Get as good as you can at your instrument, your song writing, and question it all the time.

I mean, Jimmy Page – you mentioned Led Zeppelin, I know that he never achieved what he wanted to achieve in the studio. None of these artists fully achieved it. It was always the striving to get that perfection, and that's what makes for great music and great artists.

What do you look for in artists you choose to work with?

Sometimes it tends to be the other way around these days. Artists choose me, but I'm always looking for a great song. I'm always looking for a great musician. Of course I'm always thinking "Is this going to be the new Beatles?" The new Led Zeppelin - I would love to find. Where is the next Led Zeppelin? Where is a band that even sounds anything like Led Zeppelin or Bad Company or any of the great bands from the 60′s or 70′s? They just don't seem to exist. They don't seem to stay together long enough to fully exist anyway. I mean, bands are really difficult to be in and difficult to get along with if you're a member of a band so it takes a lot of work to make a band successful and I don't think people work at it enough.

Basically, I try to clear my head and I listen to the artist hoping it's going to be something I like and something I think I can add to; that's more the case. If a band or an artist does come up and their sound is great and everything seems fine, the arrangement is all there and there's not much for me to do then that's great, but obviously not great from my point of view.

So, I'm looking for all sorts of things when I listen to a new artist for the first time. Working with Music XRay, I'm working with bands from Australia, the U.S, Canada, South America, South Africa, all over the world really. There does seem to be a common element in music when it comes to rock music. We all seem to like the same things. That is a great feeling, really. Coming up to nearly 60 years old, it's not something I imagined would happen. None of us imagined when we were in our 20′s that the new generation would in any way like the music that we liked. To be in this era where everybody writes down their favourite band and its Led Zeppelin and we're still talking about bands and rock music. It's a great thing, really, and I'm just happy to be in it.

Very few people seem to understand the music industry. Can you leave us with some advice for anyone looking to follow their dreams and make music their career?

It's a very wide subject, isn't it (the music industry)? I do Skype conferences with music students of all ages, but people seem to wait until older and older ages before they even start to learn. I say it's best to start as early as possible. I started in the music business when I was 15 and I don't think you can start early enough. I also think that it's important to know as early as possible which area of the music business that you want to join, and to get into that and to learn all about that and not try to learn every facet of it or learn what everyone else's jobs are. Admittedly, if you want to become a record producer it's good to learn engineering. It's good to be grounded in that, but if you know that you're a great guitarist and you love playing guitar I think it's best to stick to learning that instrument and doing it the best you can.

Jimmy Page, I mean, he was one of the top session musicians at age 15 or 16. He had been playing since he was a little boy. He wanted to play that guitar and know absolutely everything about it. Of course, he became a really good record producer and got into that side of things, but still, he was learning and wanted to put together a great band. A lot of the musicians that I've worked with…Paul Rogers just wanted to be a great singer. I find that some of the new bands that are great tend to specialize. Coming back to the question, that's what I think. It's good to find out early on what you're going to be best at and then honing in on that. Obviously if it's a musician then that's getting together with other musicians, getting your craft together, writing great songs.

People tend to work on their own too much these days. Sometimes you can't do everything yourself. Sometimes you're going to need a lyricist even if you're a great songwriter like Elton John. His lyrics weren't good at all when I first worked with him before he met Bernie Taupin. Sometimes you have to work with others in order to get it even better. It's a great music industry, still. Get into it as soon as possible, I say.

To get in touch with Stuart Epps regarding your music, please visit:

Stuart's official website - www.stuartepps.co.uk

Stuart's Music XRay profile - www.musicxray.com/profiles/943

IN CLOSING

You're guaranteed to get results when you put honest (meaning, not spamming. Honest, professional communication) work into the promotion of your music. How much results will depend on how good you are and how hard you work. I wish you the best, and hope you get in touch with your success stories and feedback.

You can reach James Moore and Independent Music Promotions at *yourbandisavirus@gmail.com or james@independentmusicpromotions.com, and through his website at www.independentmusicpromotions.com.*

YOUR BAND IS A VIRUS!

Made in the USA
San Bernardino, CA
26 December 2012